Cryptocurrency Market Forecasting With Catboost Models

Authored by

Heng Chen
Department of Marketing
Northern Arizona University
Arizona, United States

Cryptocurrency Market Forecasting With Catboost Models

Author: Heng Chen

ISBN (Online): 978-981-5305-51-7

ISBN (Print): 978-981-5305-52-4

ISBN (Paperback): 978-981-5305-53-1

First published in 2025.

Bentham Science Publishers Pte. Ltd.
80 Robinson Road #02-00
Singapore 068898
Singapore
Email: subscriptions@benthamscience.net

BENTHAM SCIENCE

CONTENTS

Preface

In the rapidly evolving world of finance, the advent of cryptocurrencies has introduced new dynamics that are transforming the landscape at an unprecedented pace. This book, "Cryptocurrency Market Forecasting with Catboost Models," seeks to delve into the intricate relationship between advanced machine learning techniques and the volatile cryptocurrency market. As we explore the potential of Catboost models—a machine learning algorithm renowned for its handling of categorical data—this text aims to equip financial technologists, data scientists, and market analysts with the knowledge to harness predictive analytics in cryptocurrency markets effectively.

The journey of this book is laid out to bridge theoretical concepts with practical applications, providing a comprehensive guide from basic introductions to sophisticated modeling strategies. The content is structured to guide readers through understanding the underlying principles of machine learning, focusing on the Catboost algorithm, and applying these concepts to predict market behaviors accurately. This blend of theory and application is intended to demystify the complexities of both cryptocurrency markets and advanced data modeling techniques.

As the financial sector continues to intertwine with cutting-edge technological advancements, the need for a deeper understanding of these tools becomes imperative. "Cryptocurrency Market Forecasting with Catboost Models" is not just a technical manual but a beacon for future and current professionals who aspire to innovate and lead in the digital finance era. Through this book, we invite you to explore the robust capabilities of Catboost models and their impact on cryptocurrency forecasting, providing you with the skills to make informed decisions in an increasingly digital economic environment.

Heng Chen
Department of Marketing
Northern Arizona University
Arizona, United States

CHAPTER 1

Financial Technology Trends and Cryptocurrency Dynamics

Abstract: Chapter 1 of "Cryptocurrency Market Forecasting with Catboost Models" explores the role of FinTech in transforming the financial sector through advanced technologies like blockchain, AI, and IoT. It discusses how these technologies enhance efficiency, accessibility, and economic growth, focusing mainly on their application in financial services and market forecasting.

Keywords: Artificial intelligence, Blockchain, Catboost models, Cryptocurrency, Digital transformation, FinTech, Financial services, Internet of things, Market forecasting.

INTRODUCTION

A notable change has occurred in the financial industry due to the rapid integration of FinTech. In this section, we explore pivotal technologies poised to reshape financial services, including blockchain, artificial intelligence (AI), and the Internet of Things (IoT), alongside their impact on market dynamics (Baruník and Křehlík, 2018; Gomber *et al.*, 2018; Zaki., 2019). This discussion lays the groundwork for subsequent research into the effective application of Catboost in cryptocurrency market forecasting (Derbentsev *et al.*, 2020; Livieris *et al.*, 2021; Sebastião and Godinho, 2021; Ye *et al.*, 2022). The infusion of financial technology within the sector has redefined traditional operational mechanisms and service delivery, spurred by innovations in blockchain, AI, and IoT (Singh *et al.*, 2020). This convergence has not only boosted operational efficiencies but has also expanded the range of financial services and products accessible to both consumers and businesses. Despite these significant advancements, challenges persist in harnessing these technologies for areas such as cryptocurrency market forecasting, where market dynamics are notably complex and constantly evolving. These innovations have fundamentally altered traditional financial operations and services, driving forward both innovation and the diversification of financial products available.

Heng Chen

Recent studies have begun to recognize the potential of these technologies in financial applications, but they often fail to fully integrate them into predictive models that can handle the chaotic nature of cryptocurrency markets (Abad-Segura *et al.*, 2020; Hashemi *et al.*, 2020; Wu and Duan., 2019). For instance, recent publications have demonstrated isolated applications of blockchain for transaction security and quantum computing for data encryption (Dasgupta *et al.*, 2019; Leng *et al.*, 2020; Mosteanu and Faccia., 2021). This research builds on these findings by synthesizing them into a cohesive predictive model that leverages both technologies to forecast market trends with greater precision.

This research aims to bridge these gaps by employing quantum computing and blockchain technology—areas that remain underexplored in current financial prediction models. By integrating these technologies, this study addresses the critical need for processing power and security, which are paramount when dealing with large, volatile cryptocurrency data sets. The application of quantum computing in this research allows for handling complex computations at unprecedented speeds, significantly enhancing predictive accuracy and efficiency. Concurrently, blockchain technology ensures the integrity and transparency of the predictive data used, which is crucial for maintaining trust in automated financial predictions.

Moreover, the interdisciplinary approach adopted in this study, which incorporates psychological and geopolitical analyses into the predictive models, introduces a novel layer of complexity to the existing methods. By understanding the impacts of investor behavior and global economic changes on market movements, this model offers a more comprehensive view of market dynamics, distinguishing it from traditional quantitative-only approaches.

This study not only fills a significant gap in the existing literature by providing a holistic and technologically advanced method for predicting cryptocurrency markets but also sets a new standard for how complex market dynamics can be understood and anticipated in financial technology research.

Entering the Future of Financial Technology

A digital transition is taking place in the finance industry, driven by the introduction of new technologies, greater effectiveness, greater availability, and economic growth. Let's look at some of the new developments at FinTech and predict what they'll do in the future.

What is Financial Technology (FinTech)?

The FinTech Integration Technique is being introduced in the finance sector, which is designed to simplify manual work and paper, making it easier and more efficient to manage finance. It covers a broad spectrum of applications, from e-commerce and online banking to innovative blockchain platforms and artificial intelligence-based finance sources. This has changed how clients interact with financial services, and has encouraged financial firms to invest in FinTech. Its ubiquitous and seamless integration into everyday life makes it easy to make purchases on the Internet through fast balance checks, and contactless payments. With the development of FinTech, there is a great prospect for finance.

The development of new technologies has a profound impact on the financial sector, and there are many examples of its use. Numerous R&D tax credit claims for FinTech may involve the combination of these technologies:

Internet of Things (IoT)

The Internet of Things refers to the connection of physical equipment and items to the Internet so that they can collect and exchange information. The Internet of Things is essential to deliver real-time data and to improve decision-making in the financial sector. This technique allows for the development of intelligent payment terminals that can gather information on client behaviour, determine peak trading time, and monitor equipment health. This information is used by financial institutions to optimise their business, improve their customer service, and reduce the risk of fraud. Analysis of trade patterns, for instance, helps to detect unusual activities that might indicate fraud.

Artificial Intelligence (AI)

A critical element is the use of artificial intelligence to analyze, automate, and make financial decisions. Consider chatbots on banking applications and websites; most of them use AI-powered chatbots to respond to clients' queries and provide help. This technique makes it possible for a computer to perform tasks that normally require the use of a person's brain. Using NLP and Machine Learning Algorithms, these chatbots are able to efficiently understand and react to a user's question. AI-driven robots, which are capable of handling routine tasks like checking the account balance and clarifying the transaction, can reduce manpower and speed up the reaction time, thereby greatly improving the service of the client.

Blockchain Technology

Blockchain is a distributed and distributed accounting technique that provides security, transparency, and tamper-resistant record keeping. It is the foundational technology for cryptocurrencies like Bitcoins and Ethereum, allowing secure and transparent P2P transactions without an intermediary like a bank. Apart from the fact that it can be applied to cryptographic products, the blockchain technique is also being studied for other applications, such as intelligent contracts. Such contracts will automatically implement and implement the clauses of a contract, which could revolutionize the way in which a contract is administered and performed.

Machine Learning

Using Machine Learning in finance includes the development of a Block Chain Technique, which enables a lot of data to be analysed and a person's or company's creditability to be identified without a clear program. Based on transaction history, consumption patterns, and nontraditional data sources, they provide a more accurate and dynamic rating.

As shown in Table **1**, four technologies are transforming the financial industry: the Internet of Things (IoT), Artificial Intelligence (AI), Blockchain, and Machine Learning. IoT connects physical devices to the internet to collect real-time data, improving decision-making and reducing fraud risk. AI uses machine learning and natural language processing to automate financial decisions and customer interactions, enhancing service efficiency. Blockchain is a decentralized, secure ledger system foundational to cryptocurrencies, increasing transaction security and efficiency. Machine Learning analyzes large datasets to predict creditworthiness and other financial metrics, driving personalized financial solutions and risk assessment. These technologies are advancing the financial sector by improving efficiency, security, and customer engagement.

Table 1. Technologies transforming the financial industry.

Technology	Description	Impact on Finance
Internet of Things (IoT)	Connects physical devices to the internet to collect and exchange data. Used to improve decision-making and operational efficiency.	Enables real-time data and fraud risk reduction.
Artificial Intelligence (AI)	Involves machine learning and natural language processing to automate financial decisions and customer interactions, *e.g.*, through chatbots.	Enhances service efficiency and customer interaction.

(Table 1) cont.....

Technology	Description	Impact on Finance
Blockchain	A decentralized and secure ledger system foundational to cryptocurrencies. Allows for transparent peer-to-peer transactions without intermediaries.	Increases transaction security and efficiency.
Machine Learning	Analyzes large datasets to predict and assess creditworthiness and other financial metrics without explicit programming.	Drives personalized financial solutions and risk assessment.

What are the Current Trends in FinTech?

The FinTech industry has been driven by the COVID-19 pandemic to adopt digital techniques and creativity. People sought non-contact and distant financial transactions, presenting new possibilities. But in 2023, there are many challenges facing the world's FinTech industry, including anticipated inflation, higher interest rates, geopolitical conflicts, and unexpected events such as the failure of some U.S. bank failures. Despite these obstacles, the British FinTech industry has continued to adapt and innovate. Notable developments in the financial industry are the development of Distributed Finance (DFI), increased emphasis on sustainable development, and continuous integration of artificial intelligence and blockchain techniques to increase the efficiency and security of financial transactions.

Decentralized Finance (DeFi)

Decentralized Finance (DFI) is a blockchain-driven financial system that allows automatic and distributed access to credit, loan, and trading, which allows customers to interact directly with each other, thus removing the need for brokers to make them more accessible, transparent, and autonomous. Through the use of Intelligent Contracts and Blockchain Techniques, Data Warehouse is responding to a growing demand for inclusive and effective finance in an ever more interconnected, digital world.

A Priority of Sustainability

Sustainability has been one of the main priorities at FinTech, where firms and clients are increasingly emphasizing environmentally friendly and socially aware finance practices. Businesses are adopting environmentally friendly measures like paperless trading and green technologies, which will bring their financing activities into line with the broader efforts to combat climate change and promote a sustainable future.

Our customer, who is the best example of sustainable development at FinTech, has introduced vegetarianism to the banking industry. Their vegan payment system offers a green alternative to all banking sessions. The project is eligible for the Research and Development Tax Relief and we have helped the customer get a GBP 12 000 tax rebate for its innovation in solving the technical problems.

Cybersecurity Innovation

With the development of FinTech's landscape, strong cyber security measures have come into play. To protect financial transactions and protect sensitive client data, FinTech companies have invested heavily in innovative cybersecurity solutions, including advanced cryptography, biometrics, and behavioral analysis. Using advanced AI and ML algorithms, we continually analyse large quantities of data, identify unusual trends, and anticipate potential safety hazards, which will eventually strengthen the stability of the financial system.Adaptive authentication is a powerful tool that enables dynamic analysis of user behaviour. This allows for the detection of suspicious activities and provides an extra layer of security against unauthorised access and fraud.

Embedded Finance Integration

The smooth incorporation of financial services into nonfinancial platforms is what makes embedded finance unique. The trend has enabled companies in different sectors, including electronic commerce and health care, to offer integrated finance solutions like payments, credit, and insurance on their platforms. For instance, a lot of online commerce websites are now able to provide you with a quick way to get funding at check-in, which will improve your overall shopping experience.

Central Bank Digital Currencies (CBDCs)

With increasing attention from central banks worldwide, there is growing interest in exploring the advantages of developing digital versions of their national currencies, which has resulted in rapid progress in the research and development of Central Bank Digital Currencies (CBDCs). CBDCs are able to enhance financial integration, lower transaction costs, and offer more efficient instruments for implementing monetary policy.

As shown in Table **2**, several current trends and innovations are shaping the FinTech landscape: Decentralized Finance (DeFi), Sustainability Initiatives, Cybersecurity Innovations, Embedded Finance, and Central Bank Digital Currencies (CBDCs). DeFi leverages blockchain technology to enable autonomous financial transactions, such as credit and trading, without relying on traditional intermediaries, promoting accessibility, transparency, and autonomy. Sustainability initiatives within FinTech include environmentally friendly practices like paperless transactions and green technologies, which also enhance accessibility and transparency. Cybersecurity innovations are critical for protecting financial transactions and data, employing advanced AI and machine learning techniques to enhance privacy and reduce fraud, thereby building trust. Embedded finance integrates financial services into non-financial platforms, such as e-commerce and healthcare, expanding the reach and integration of financial services. Lastly, CBDCs, the development of digital currencies by central banks, have the potential to revolutionize national and global financial infrastructures, enhancing monetary policy and financial inclusivity.

Table 2. Current trends and innovations in FinTech.

Trend/Innovation	Description	Significance in FinTech
Decentralized Finance (DeFi)	Uses blockchain to enable autonomous financial transactions and services, such as credit and trading, without traditional intermediaries.	Promotes accessibility, transparency, and autonomy.
Sustainability Initiatives	Includes environmentally friendly practices within financial operations, like paperless transactions and green technologies.	Promotes accessibility, transparency, and autonomy.
Cybersecurity Innovations	Advanced security protocols to protect financial transactions and data through AI and machine learning, enhancing privacy and reducing fraud.	Critical for protecting data integrity and building trust.
Embedded Finance	Integration of financial services into non-financial platforms, making finance accessible through different sector interfaces like e-commerce or healthcare platforms.	Expands financial service accessibility and integration.
Central Bank Digital Currencies (CBDCs)	Exploration and development of digital currencies by central banks to enhance monetary policy implementation and financial inclusivity.	Potentially revolutionizes national and global financial infrastructures.

Integration of Robotics with Traditional Financial Processes

Integration of robotics into FinTech is an obvious trend driven by the need for more automated and more efficient financial processes. Robots, which are used by FinTech firms to enhance customer service, data input, and fraud detection, have been identified as contributing to faster and more accurate results. Robotic Process Automation (RPA) is an excellent case in that it automates regular, rules-based work and enables the financial sector to concentrate more on sophisticated services. In addition, robot advisers are becoming more and more popular, offering customers automatic, algorithmic investment strategies.

What Industry Challenges Does Financial Technology Solve?

Revolutionizing the financial landscape, FinTech has made it more accessible, efficient, and secure for both individuals and businesses. Here are the challenges it faces:

- Financial Technology (finTech) has increased the availability of finance by providing services and resources to those who are under-represented or marginalised by the conventional banking system.
- Operational Inefficiencies: FinTech streamlines operations by automating and digitizing activities, cutting down on manual work, and increasing productivity.
- FinTech, which offers a cost-effective substitute for conventional finance, can ease the financial burden of customers by avoiding expensive transaction costs.
- FinTech firms have made significant investments in cyber security to protect financial transactions and protect the confidentiality of clients' data. Advanced verification techniques and sophisticated fraud detection systems make the finance environment more secure.
- While there are limits to creativity in conventional banking, FinTech is making a big splash by challenging established banking standards. By introducing new finance products and services, start-ups as well as established Fintech firms are pushing for adaptation and transformation.
- Slow and Complex Payment Systems - Fast and Efficient Payments - Fast and Fast Money Delivery - Faster and More Efficient Payments, Fast Cash Transfers and Immediate Cash Transfers.
- Financial Literacy and Learning: Many of the Fintech applications have user-friendly interfaces that provide learning tools that enhance awareness about finance and allow consumers to make informed finance decisions.
- The application of RegTech in the fintech industry facilitates regulatory compliance by simplifying and automating compliance processes so as to ensure compliance with complex rules and avoid possible sanctions.

What are the Predictions for Financial Technology (FinTech)?

As specialists in R&D tax credit, we collaborate closely with a variety of FinTech companies and startups that have achieved unprecedented success. Some are more established than others, conducting R&D on the side of their main business operations. We observe the FinTech trends in real time and gain insight from the experts as to what they will be working on next. Our team has compiled what we deem to be the FinTech trends for the coming year:

An Acceleration of Biometrics Adoption

Biometrics includes the use of distinctive physical properties or behaviour, such as fingerprints, facial features, or speech patterns, to identify and permit access to persons. It offers more secure security than PINs or passwords. Now that face recognition has been incorporated into modern smartphones, it is expected to be used by the finance industry to improve the safety of sensitive data.

The use of biometrics in the financial sector will bring about a revolution in the safety of the system, replacing the traditional authentication methods and lowering the risk of identity theft. The switch to biometric security strengthens the security of the transaction and improves the user's experience by providing a smooth and efficient authentication system.

Recently, there has been an increasing focus on the improvement of biometrics, which should be introduced in finance. At its annual conference in Dec. 2023, AWS, the leading cloud-based firm, launched a state-of-the-art security system called Amazon One Enterprise. In the future, we might be able to use this technique to pay rather than a conventional bank or cell phone.

The Gamification of Finance

The implementation of game-like functions like scoring, challenges, and prizes in noncompetitive settings is called "Gamification", which encourages participation and interaction. It gives the user a sense of achievement and keeps them interested. Additionally, it removes the intimidation factor related to personal finance and investment and serves as a learning tool to help individuals make smart financial decisions.

Banking application, which keeps people on the move and helps them live, has been introduced into the digital banking industry like the virtual piggy bank. It tells them what they have to pay every week to achieve their savings target, so they can monitor the impact of their contributions on time. Mario's tags, unlocking your savings target, sharing your account with a friend, *etc.*, are some of the special benefits that encourage you to invest more in digital banking.

It is expected that the company will include game-like elements in its apps, thus creating a more informed and committed user group.

Buy Now Pay Later (BNPL) Initiatives

It is expected that this forecast will spread and develop over the next 12 months. Buy Now, Pay Later Plans allow the client to buy immediately and delay the payment for some time, often *via* an installment scheme, rather than creating the usual credit card debt.

As the cost of living keeps growing, more people are switching to paying schemes, which is why we expect them to grow by 2024. Most Gen Zellers depend on Buy Now Pay Later, like Klarna and Clearpay, to keep up with the latest fashion and technological developments.

We believe that more rules will be put in place to avoid unlimited lending and default; we expect a new set of rules to emerge.

More extensive use of BNPL will probably go hand in hand with improvements such as personalised payment plans, better user interfaces, and cooperation among financial firms with a wider audience for BNPL.

Cyber security capability will be enhanced in parallel with the spread of cloud adoption within finance.

Many of the techniques discussed in this paper depend on the cloud. And as FinTech progresses, so does the use of cloud services. Cloud makes it possible for a financial organization to realize a simplified scale at the same time as cutting costs. Nonetheless, robust cyber security protocols are needed to deal with and manage the security problems resulting from the integration of FinTech with cloud technology.

The growing emphasis on productivity, scalability, and team building will drive cyber security development. Also, firms will give priority to security measures that are tailored to the cloud-based financial system. That would require more investment in sophisticated cryptography, detecting threats, and securing cloud infrastructure to protect the privacy and integrity of data stored and processed in the cloud.

FinTech will Revolutionize Everyday Operations

This tendency has been easily incorporated into nonfinancial platforms and apps, providing customers with better and more simplified access to payments, loans, and finance management tools. Look forward to a wide range of services incorporating finTech functionality, ranging from e-commerce websites to health care systems, because this industry places user comfort and efficiency first.

Data Analytics

The FinTech sector is projected to grow dramatically by 2024, where it will be crucial for decision-making, personalised finance, and managing risk. In order to obtain actionable insights, improve customer experiences through tailored offerings, and refine prediction models for evaluating financial risks, FinTech firms are increasingly making use of large datasets. The combination of large data and analysis, combined with their enhanced capabilities, is poised to change the way they operate and build a more data-driven, effective, and customer-oriented environment in an ever changing global financial technology landscape.

CONCLUSION

This chapter has explored the transformative impact of cutting-edge technologies such as AI, blockchain, and IoT on the financial sector. By enhancing security, efficiency, and accessibility, these technologies not only redefine how financial services operate but also provide profound insights into market trends and behaviors. These insights are crucial for developing robust models for cryptocurrency market forecasting, an area that remains pivotal as the financial landscape continues to evolve.

As we look to the future, the ongoing adoption and deeper integration of these technologies will undoubtedly play a critical role in advancing financial services. However, several research pathways need to be explored to fully harness their potential:

- **Integration and Interoperability:** Future research should focus on the integration and interoperability of these technologies. How can blockchain, AI, and IoT work in a more synergistic manner to provide even greater improvements in the financial sector? Research could explore frameworks that facilitate seamless data flow and interaction between these technologies to enhance predictive analytics and cybersecurity.
- **Advanced Predictive Models:** While we have begun to tap into the potential of these technologies for market forecasting, there is a substantial scope for the development of more advanced predictive models. Future studies could focus on utilizing deep learning and complex machine learning models that can handle the vast amounts of data generated by IoT devices and blockchain transactions, providing more accurate and timely market predictions.
- **Regulatory and Ethical Implications:** The rapid advancement and integration of these technologies also bring forth significant regulatory and ethical implications that need to be addressed. Future research should explore the regulatory frameworks necessary to govern the use of these technologies in finance. Additionally, studies on the ethical implications of automated decision-making systems in finance would provide valuable insights into developing responsible AI systems.

- **Enhancing Security Features:** As the financial sector becomes increasingly digitized, security concerns become more pronounced. Future research should explore advanced cryptographic techniques and blockchain solutions to enhance data security and privacy. Investigating quantum-resistant blockchain technologies could be particularly pertinent as quantum computing becomes more mainstream.
- **Economic Impact Studies:** It is crucial to understand the broader economic impacts of integrating these technologies into the financial sector. Future research could examine how blockchain, AI, and IoT influence economic policies, financial stability, and global financial inclusion, especially in underdeveloped and developing regions.
- **Scalability Solutions:** As these technologies continue to be adopted, scalability becomes a critical issue. Research into new algorithms and architectures that enhance the scalability of blockchain and IoT systems without compromising on speed or security would be highly beneficial.
- **Sustainable Practices:** Finally, as the global emphasis on sustainability grows, future research should also focus on how fintech can contribute to environmentally friendly practices. This could include studies on energy-efficient blockchain technologies, AI applications for reducing paper use, and IoT solutions for enhancing energy efficiency in financial operations.

By pursuing these research pathways, we can ensure that the integration of AI, blockchain, and IoT not only transforms the financial sector but does so in a way that is secure, efficient, and inclusive. This will pave the way for a more robust and innovative financial landscape, well-equipped to face the challenges of the future.

REFERENCES

Abad-Segura, E., González-Zamar, M.D., López-Meneses, E., Vázquez-Cano, E. (2020). Financial technology: review of trends, approaches and management. *Mathematics, 8*(6), 951. [http://dx.doi.org/10.3390/math8060951]

Baruník, J., Křehlík, T. (2018). Measuring the frequency dynamics of financial connectedness and systemic risk. *J. Financ. Econom., 16*(2), 271-296. [http://dx.doi.org/10.1093/jjfinec/nby001]

Dasgupta, D., Shrein, J.M., Gupta, K.D. (2019). A survey of blockchain from security perspective. *Journal of Banking and Financial Technology, 3*(1), 1-17. [http://dx.doi.org/10.1007/s42786-018-00002-6]

Derbentsev, V., Matviychuk, A., Soloviev, V. N. (2020). Forecasting of cryptocurrency prices using machine learning. *Advanced studies of financial technologies and cryptocurrency markets,* 211-231. [http://dx.doi.org/10.1007/978-981-15-4498-9_12]

Gomber, P., Kauffman, R.J., Parker, C., Weber, B.W. (2018). On the fintech revolution: Interpreting the forces of innovation, disruption, and transformation in financial services. *J. Manage. Inf. Syst., 35*(1), 220-265. [http://dx.doi.org/10.1080/07421222.2018.1440766]

Hashemi Joo, M., Nishikawa, Y., Dandapani, K. (2019). Cryptocurrency, a successful application of blockchain technology. *Manag. Finance, 46*(6), 715-733. [http://dx.doi.org/10.1108/MF-09-2018-0451]

Leng, J., Zhou, M., Zhao, J.L., Huang, Y., Bian, Y. (2022). Blockchain security: A survey of techniques and research directions. *IEEE Trans. Serv. Comput., 15*(4), 2490-2510. [http://dx.doi.org/10.1109/TSC.2020.3038641]

Livieris, I.E., Kiriakidou, N., Stavroyiannis, S., Pintelas, P. (2021). An advanced CNN-LSTM model for cryptocurrency forecasting. *Electronics (Basel), 10*(3), 287. [http://dx.doi.org/10.3390/electronics10030287]

Mosteanu, N.R., Faccia, A. (2021). Fintech frontiers in quantum computing, fractals, and blockchain distributed ledger: Paradigm shifts and open innovation. *J. Open Innov., 7*(1), 19. [http://dx.doi.org/10.3390/joitmc7010019]

Sebastião, H., Godinho, P. (2021). Forecasting and trading cryptocurrencies with machine learning under changing market conditions. *Financial Innovation, 7*(1), 3. [http://dx.doi.org/10.1186/s40854-020-00217-x] [PMID: 35024269]

Singh, S., Sharma, P.K., Yoon, B., Shojafar, M., Cho, G.H., Ra, I.H. (2020). Convergence of blockchain and artificial intelligence in IoT network for the sustainable smart city. *Sustain Cities Soc., 63*, 102364. [http://dx.doi.org/10.1016/j.scs.2020.102364]

Wu, B., Duan, T. (2019). The application of blockchain technology in financial markets. *J. Phys. Conf. Ser., 1176*(4), 042094. [http://dx.doi.org/10.1088/1742-6596/1176/4/042094]

Ye, X., Li, Y., Feng, X., Heng, C. (2022). A crypto market forecasting method based on Catboost model and bigdata. *7th International Conference on Intelligent Computing and Signal Processing (ICSP),* 686-689. [http://dx.doi.org/10.1109/ICSP54964.2022.9778789]

Zaki, M. (2019). Digital transformation: harnessing digital technologies for the next generation of services. *J. Serv. Mark., 33*(4), 429-435. [http://dx.doi.org/10.1108/JSM-01-2019-0034]

CHAPTER 2

Catboost Model Unveiled

Abstract: This chapter delves into the Catboost algorithm, a machine learning method renowned for its handling of categorical data through gradient boosting techniques. It provides an in-depth analysis of Catboost's capabilities, contrasts it with other machine learning algorithms, and discusses its applications across various industries.

Keywords: Catboost, Categorical data, Gradient boosting, Hyperparameter tuning, Machine learning, Overfitting, Predictive modeling, Supervised learning.

INTRODUCTION

Catboost stands out in the field of machine learning for its specialized handling of categorical data, offering native support and efficient data processing without extensive preprocessing. This chapter introduces the foundational aspects of the Catboost algorithm, explains its significance in handling categorical features and discusses its advantages over other algorithms like XGBoost and LightGBM.

Recent studies have further emphasized the importance of efficiently processing categorical data, which is often cumbersome and error-prone in traditional machine-learning workflows (Ahmed *et al.*, 2020; Gudivada *et al.*, 2017; Tatineni and Boppana, 2021). Researchers have noted that preprocessing techniques can distort the natural structure of data and lead to suboptimal models (Zhu *et al.*, 2018). CatBoost's approach eliminates these steps by intelligently transforming categorical variables into numerical counterparts internally, thus preserving data integrity and speeding up the learning process.

The innovation of CatBoost lies in its method of combining gradient boosting with an ordered boosting mechanism and a novel algorithm for processing categorical data. Unlike its predecessors, which often require detailed tuning of parameters to handle overfitting, CatBoost introduces ordered boosting to prevent this common issue effectively. This approach not only enhances model accuracy but also provides a robust framework that performs consistently across different datasets and domains.

Heng Chen

This chapter delves into these aspects, setting the stage for a detailed exploration of CatBoost's capabilities and its practical applications across various industries. By integrating recent advancements and presenting new methodologies, it aims to provide a comprehensive overview that underscores the unique contributions of CatBoost to the field of machine learning.

MACHINE LEARNING PRIMER: A FIRST ENCOUNTER WITH CATBOOST

CatBoost is an open-source, gradient-boosting machine learning algorithm developed by Yandex, specifically designed for efficient handling of categorical features, a Russian multinational company specializing in Internet-related products and services. The name CatBoost is derived from two words, 'Category' and 'Boosting'. It is designed to handle categorical variables, which are a common occurrence in many data science problems.

CatBoost (Categorical Boosting) is an advanced open-source machine learning algorithm developed by Yandex that specializes in gradient boosting techniques. It is particularly renowned for its efficiency in handling categorical data directly, eliminating the need for extensive preprocessing that other machine learning models often require. This feature makes CatBoost unique among gradient boosting frameworks such as XGBoost and LightGBM.

Core Features of CatBoost

Direct Handling of Categorical Data: Unlike other algorithms that require categorical data to be preprocessed into numerical format, CatBoost handles categorical variables natively using a technique called contrast target encoding.

Ordered Boosting: This feature helps combat overfitting by avoiding the leakage of target information during the training process. It ensures that each tree is built using a different permutation of data.

Symmetric Tree Growth: CatBoost grows trees depth-wise, making balanced trees, which helps in reducing bias and variance.

CatBoost improves the model iteratively by sequentially adding new trees that correct the mistakes of the previously built trees. The specific formula is as follows:

- Initialization

$$f_0(x) = \beta$$

Where β is the initial prediction for all instances, usually the average of the target values.

- For each iteration t, update the model:

$$f_t(x) = f_{t-1}(x) + \gamma_t h_t(x)$$

Where y_t is the learning rate, $h_t(x)$ is the new tree, and $f_{t-1}(x)$ is the prediction from the previous model.

- Learning the tree involves minimizing the loss:

$$L = \sum_{i=1}^{n} l\,(y_i, f_{t-1}(x_i) + h_t(x_i))$$

Where l is the loss function, y_t is the target value, $f_{t-1}(x_i)$ is the cumulative prediction from the previous model, and $h_t(x_i)$) is the prediction of the new tree.

As shown in Table **3**, a comparison of CatBoost, XGBoost, and LightGBM highlights the specific advantages of CatBoost in several key areas. CatBoost automatically handles categorical data without the need for manual preprocessing, unlike XGBoost and LightGBM, which both require one-hot encoding. Additionally, CatBoost uses ordered boosting to reduce overfitting, while XGBoost requires careful tuning to prevent overfitting, and LightGBM is prone to overfitting, particularly with small datasets. In terms of performance efficiency, CatBoost offers efficient use of default parameters, requiring less extensive hyperparameter tuning compared to XGBoost and LightGBM. CatBoost also has comprehensive GPU support for faster model training, outpacing XGBoost and LightGBM in this area. In terms of predictive performance, CatBoost often outperforms other models, especially when working with categorical data. The ease of model training is also a key advantage of CatBoost, as it requires fewer parameters and manages categorical data more effectively. Finally, CatBoost's symmetric tree growth algorithm helps reduce bias and variance, unlike the greedy or leaf-wise algorithms used by XGBoost and LightGBM, respectively.

Table 3. Comparison table that highlights the specific advantages of CatBoost over XGBoost and LightGBM.

Feature	CatBoost	XGBoost	LightGBM	Feature
Handling of Categorical Data	Automatically processes categorical features without manual preprocessing.	Requires manual preprocessing like one-hot encoding.	Requires manual preprocessing like one-hot encoding.	**Handling of Categorical Data**

(Table 3) cont.....

Feature	CatBoost	XGBoost	LightGBM	Feature
Reduction of Overfitting	Uses ordered boosting to train each tree on a randomly permuted order of data, reducing overfitting.	Uses regularization and other techniques but may still overfit without careful tuning.	Prone to overfitting without careful tuning, especially on small datasets.	**Reduction of Overfitting**
Performance Efficiency	Efficient use of default parameters, less need for extensive hyperparameter tuning.	Often requires significant hyperparameter tuning to achieve optimal performance.	Often requires significant hyperparameter tuning to achieve optimal performance, though it is generally faster at training.	**Performance Efficiency**
GPU Support	Comprehensive GPU support for faster model training.	Has GPU support, but it may not be as efficient as CatBoost's implementation.	Limited GPU support, mainly optimized for faster training on CPUs.	**GPU Support**
Predictive Performance	Often outperforms others in empirical tests, especially with categorical data.	Strong performance, but sometimes less effective with categorical data.	Fast training with large datasets but may underperform with categorical data compared to CatBoost.	**Predictive Performance**
Ease of Model Training	More straightforward model training due to better handling of categorical data and fewer parameters.	Requires more careful management of learning rate and tree characteristics.	Requires tuning of more hyperparameters, especially for large data sets.	**Ease of Model Training**
Tree Growth Algorithm	Symmetric tree growth helps reduce bias and variance.	Greedy algorithm that chooses the best split based on predefined criteria.	Leaf-wise growth, can lead to more complex models and potential overfitting.	**Tree Growth Algorithm**

This algorithm is regarded as the gold standard in dealing with categorical features in machine learning problems due to its superior performance. CatBoost can handle categorical variables by transforming them into numbers, thereby eliminating the need for extensive data preprocessing seen in other machine learning models. Moreover, it can handle a large number of categorical features effortlessly, making it a go-to algorithm for challenges with significant categorical data.

CatBoost also leverages gradient boosting on decision trees, which is a powerful machine-learning technique. With its robust and scalable handling of categorical features, great accuracy, and efficient speed, CatBoost indeed sets the gold standard for handling categorical data in the field of machine learning.

CatBoost offers several powerful features and capabilities that distinguish it from other boosting algorithm frameworks. Here are some of its notable features and key advantages:

Support for categorical features: Handling categorical variables is often a three-step process involving transformation, combination, and then application of a machine learning algorithm. CatBoost simplifies this to a great extent by offering native support for categorical variables. With this capability, it can automatically convert categorical variables into numbers, allowing data scientists to bypass the cumbersome steps of manual preprocessing.

Robust overfitting handling: Overfitting is a common problem in machine learning models, where algorithms perform well on training data but poorly on unseen data. CatBoost uses the Ordered Boosting technique, which helps reduce the risk of overfitting and makes the model robust.

Excellent performance with default parameters: CatBoost outshines many popular boosting methods when used with default parameters. This means that, in many cases, extensive hyperparameter tuning might not be necessary, simplifying the model-training process significantly.

GPU training: CatBoost also supports GPU acceleration, which results in faster computation. This feature comes in handy when dealing with large datasets, where the training time can significantly be reduced by running computations on the GPU.

Model interpretation tools: CatBoost provides tools for interpretation, including SHAP values and feature importance, to help understand how the model makes decisions and to identify the most influential features.

CatBoost, given its versatility and strong performance, is widely used across various industries and for diverse applications. Here are some key scenarios:

Search Ranking: In platforms like e-commerce, search engines, and booking websites, items need to be ranked based on relevance to the user's search query. CatBoost can effectively model the complex relationships between features in these ranking problems due to its robust handling of categorical variables and ordered boosting features.

Personalized Recommendations: Recommender systems in music platforms, video streaming services, and e-commerce sites often deal with a large number of categorical variables, such as user and item IDs. CatBoost's strength in handling categorical variables makes it ideally suited for such problems.

Predictive Modelling: Applications such as demand forecasting, customer lifetime value prediction, and health outcome prediction often deal with a mix of numerical and categorical features. CatBoost's ability to handle such data natively makes it a powerful tool for predictive modeling.

Fraud Detection: In sectors like banking and insurance, the need to detect fraudulent transactions or claims is paramount. These often involve dealing with a large number of categorical features, such as transaction IDs, user details, and location details. CatBoost's superior performance with categorical features makes it well-suited to detect patterns that could indicate fraudulent behavior.

CatBoost spans many domains and can address a variety of problems. Its robust handling of categorical features and strong accuracy performance make it a viable choice for a wide range of machine learning tasks.

Comparing CatBoost with other popular gradient boosting methods such as XGBoost and LightGBM reveals significant advantages it brings to the table (Fig. **1**).

Handling Categorical Features: Traditional gradient boosting frameworks like XGBoost and LightGBM require explicit preprocessing of categorical data into a numerical format which can often be time-consuming. CatBoost, on the other hand, offers in-built handling of categorical features, resulting in not just a time-efficient process but often also better model performance.

Avoiding Overfitting: Overfitting refers to a model that performs well on training data but poorly on unseen data. While XGBoost and LightGBM provide several parameters to control the model complexity and fight overfitting, CatBoost uses an ordered boosting process to naturally prevent overfitting providing robust performance out-of-the-box.

Prediction Accuracy: Various benchmarks show that CatBoost generally surpasses both XGBoost and LightGBM in terms of prediction accuracy when default parameters are used. This is largely due to CatBoost's advanced handling of categorical variables that other algorithms do not uniquely account for.

Ease of Use: Unlike XGBoost and LightGBM which may need extensive parameter tuning to achieve optimal performance, CatBoost often delivers superior results with default parameters, making it a simpler and more convenient solution to deploy.

In conclusion, the unique methodology employed by CatBoost for handling categorical data, preventing overfitting, and the exceptional prediction accuracy provided with the default parameters set it apart from XGBoost and LightGBM, making it a powerful choice for a broad spectrum of prediction tasks.

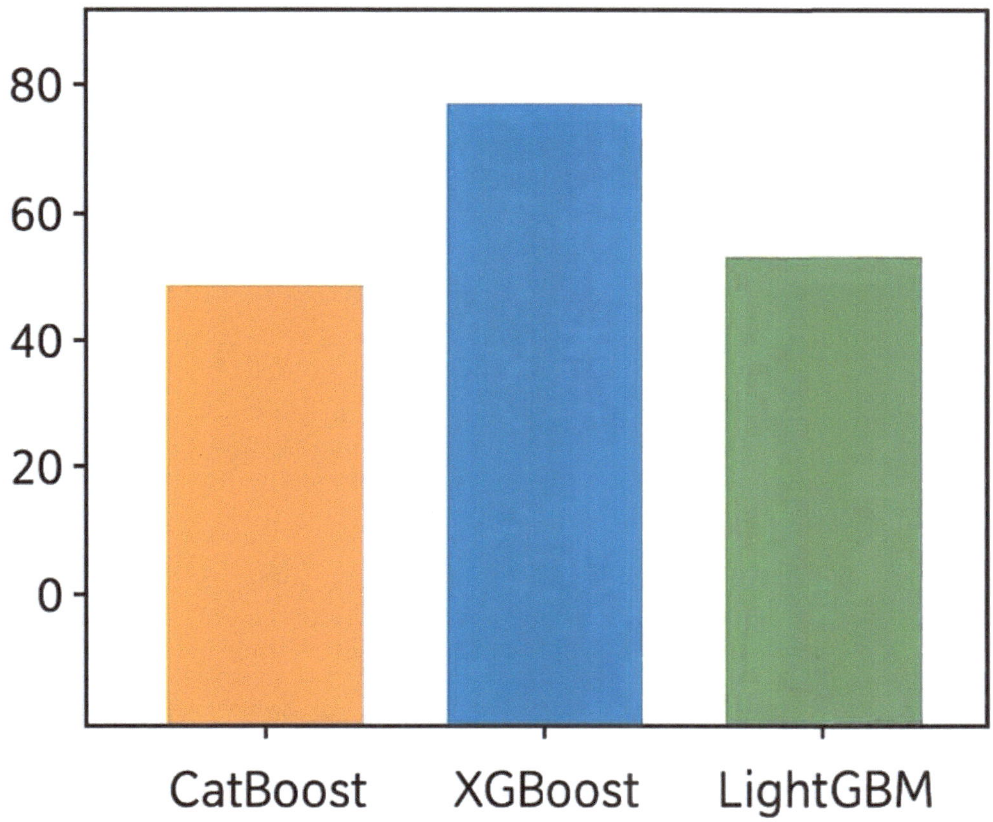

Fig. (1). Comparison of Gradient Boosting Algorithms.

A bar chart comparing the key features of CatBoost, XGBoost, and LightGBM based on simulated data. The chart rates each algorithm on categorical data handling, overfitting prevention, performance, and training speed, with scores out of 10. This visual representation highlights the strengths and weaknesses of each algorithm across different aspects.

Case Studies

Sure, let us look at the real-world application scenarios of CatBoost with the projects: mljar/mljar-supervised and ScottfreeLLC/AlphaPy.

mljar/mljar-supervised: It is an automated Machine Learning tool that is designed for data scientists' needs. It uses CatBoost in the background to handle tasks that involve a great deal of categorical features, thanks to CatBoost's superior categorical feature handling capability. It helped to enhance the overall workflow and provided more accurate models on varied datasets. It reveals CatBoost's practical utility in delivering effective solutions that cater to categorical data.

ScottfreeLLC/AlphaPy: AlphaPy is a machine learning framework for both speculators and data scientists to create a winning, automated trading system. It extensively uses CatBoost owing to its default hyperparameters that outperform other models. It offers a model stack including logistic regression, random forests, gradient boosting machines, support vector machines, and neural networks. CatBoost provides a higher predictive accuracy potential that underpins AlphaPy's deployment.

Conclusion and Further Reading

By incorporating CatBoost, both projects successfully delivered their tasks with better efficiency and accuracy. These use cases depict how CatBoost can be employed within a larger framework to leverage its strengths, such as superior categorical features handling and predictive accuracy.

In conclusion, CatBoost distinguishes itself from other machine learning algorithms with its excellent support for categorical features, robust performance with default parameters, advanced overfitting prevention techniques, high prediction accuracy, and GPU training support. Its application spans various fields, from search ranking and personalized recommendations to user behavior prediction and fraud detection, demonstrating its broad adaptability and effectiveness.

Looking ahead, there remains a great deal of potential for research in several directions. For instance, research can be conducted on enhancing CatBoost's efficiency when working with truly massive datasets or expanding its application to new domains such as image or text classification. Moreover, as with any cutting-edge technology, there is always room for improvement in terms of performance optimization and ease of use.

For anyone interested in digging deeper into CatBoost, I highly recommend referring to CatBoost's official documentation on their website for a comprehensive understanding. The project's GitHub page at https://github.com/catboost/catboost can also offer more insights and learning materials. It hosts a bustling community of developers and researchers, where you can find the latest updates, ask questions, and even contribute to the project's development. So go ahead and explore the fascinating world of CatBoost!

Decoding Supervised Learning

Introduction

Supervised learning is a machine learning method in which an algorithm learns a model from labeled training data. The "label" here refers to the output we want the model to predict. Once the training is completed, we use the model to predict the labels or outputs of new or unseen input data. The accuracy of the learned model is quantified by the difference between predicted and actual labels in the test data.

The importance of supervised learning in the field of machine learning is self-evident. It has become a fundamental machine learning technology for building applications such as email filtering, fraud detection, sales forecasting, and medical diagnosis.

Regarding the basic working principle, the supervised learning process starts with a set of training data containing features (or input variables) and their corresponding labels (or output variables). The model learns the mapping between these features and labels, and summarizes this mapping as predicting labels for unseen data.

Supervised learning is mainly divided into classification and regression problems. Classification problems involve predicting discrete categories or categories. For example, determining whether an email is spam or whether a tumor is malignant. Regression problems involve predicting continuous numerical values, such as predicting house prices or stock values.

In both classification and regression, our goal is to build a model that accurately maps input features to output labels. For new and unprecedented data, if a model can make more accurate predictions, then the model is considered more effective.

Key Concepts

Some core concepts in supervised learning include:

Features: Features are the individual measurable properties or characteristics of a phenomenon being observed. In machine learning, features are used as input variables that help the model make predictions. For example, in real estate price prediction, features might include the house's area (in square feet), number of rooms, age of the property, proximity to essential amenities, and neighborhood crime rates. The quality and relevance of features directly impact the model's ability to make accurate predictions.

Labels: Labels are the outputs or results you want to predict. In supervised learning, each training example includes one or more labels. Continuing with the house price prediction example, the label would be the actual selling price of each house. Labels are crucial as they are what the model tries to predict based on the learned patterns from features during training.

Training Set: The training set is a collection of data used to discover potentially predictive relationships. This dataset includes both input features and corresponding labels. Models learn to associate specific inputs with specific outputs during training. The size and diversity of the training set significantly influence the model's ability to generalize well to new, unseen data.

Testing Set: The testing set is a separate portion of the dataset that is used only for testing the model's performance after the model has been trained on the training set. This dataset helps evaluate how well the model has learned to generalize from the training data. It is critical for assessing the effectiveness of the model, as it simulates how the model is expected to perform in real-world applications.

Model: A model in machine learning is the output of the training process and is defined by the specific algorithm used and the set of parameters identified as being the best during the training phase. This model encapsulates what has been learned from the training data and is used to make predictions on new data. Essentially, it is the mathematical framework or equation that links the features to the target label.

Prediction: Prediction refers to the output generated by the machine learning model when it is presented with new, unseen data. After being trained on a dataset, the model uses what it has learned to predict the label of new examples. In supervised learning, the accuracy of predictions significantly affects the utility of the model in practical scenarios.

Classification: Classification is a type of supervised learning where the output variable is a category. Tasks like spam detection in emails, image recognition, and diagnosing diseases from symptoms are examples where classification models are used. The model learns to assign each input to one of the predefined categories.

Regression: Regression involves predicting a continuous quantity. Unlike classification, where the labels are discrete categories, regression models predict a continuous output. Examples of regression tasks include predicting salary based on experience and education or forecasting stock prices.

Error: The error in a machine learning context measures the discrepancy between the predicted values and the actual values in the training or testing data. There are different types of errors—like bias error and variance error—which reflect different aspects of accuracy and generalization in predictions.

Loss Function: The loss function, also known as a cost function, quantifies the difference between the predicted values and the actual values. It provides a measure of how well the model is performing. The goal of training a model is to find the set of parameters that minimize this loss function. Common examples include Mean Squared Error for regression tasks and Cross-Entropy Loss for classification tasks.

Optimization: Optimization is the process of adjusting the model parameters to minimize the loss function. This process involves techniques like gradient descent or more advanced methods such as stochastic gradient descent and Adam optimizer. The choice of optimization algorithm can affect the speed and quality of the training process.

By understanding and effectively applying these concepts, one can develop more robust, efficient, and accurate supervised learning models.

Popular Algorithms

The following are several commonly used machine learning algorithms in supervised learning tasks:

- **Linear Regression:** This algorithm models the relationship between a dependent, continuous target variable and one or more independent variables by fitting a linear equation to observed data. It assumes that the relationship between the variables is linear and uses the least squares method to minimize the error in prediction. It's particularly useful for forecasting and finding out the relative significance of variables.
- **Logistic Regression:** Logistic regression is employed for binary classification tasks where the output is categorical. It models the probability of the default class (*e.g.*, 'success' or 'failure') by fitting data to a logistic curve. It works well with binary, dichotomous variables and can be extended to multi-class classification under certain frameworks like one-vs-rest (OvR).
- **Decision Trees:** Decision trees are a non-parametric supervised learning method used for classification and regression. The model learns to make decisions based on asking a series of questions, with each node in the tree representing a feature in an instance to be classified, and the leaves representing class labels. Trees can overfit data, which is commonly handled by methods like pruning.

- **Random Forest:** An extension of decision trees, Random Forest improves prediction accuracy by building multiple decision trees and voting on the most popular output (classification) or averaging the outputs (regression). It reduces overfitting by using bootstrapping (sampling data with replacement) and feature randomness when splitting trees, enhancing model robustness.
- **K-Nearest Neighbors (K-NN):** K-NN is a type of instance-based or lazy learning where the function is only approximated locally and all computation is deferred until classification. It's particularly useful where the decision boundary is very irregular. The algorithm scales poorly with high dimension data, often addressed by dimension reduction techniques.
- **Support Vector Machines (SVM):** SVMs are powerful linear models that work by mapping data to a high-dimensional feature space where a hyperplane can be used to separate classes. SVMs can be kernelized to solve nonlinear classification problems, utilizing functions like polynomial, radial basis function (RBF), or sigmoid to enable separation in the original feature space.
- **Ensemble Methods:** Techniques like bagging and boosting are used to create a strong classifier from a number of weak models. Bagging reduces variance and helps avoid overfitting, whereas boosting focuses on reducing bias and builds models in a sequential manner where each subsequent model attempts to correct the errors made by previous models.
- **Neural Networks:** These are a set of algorithms, modeled loosely after the human brain, designed to recognize patterns. They interpret sensory data through a kind of machine perception, labeling, or clustering. Neural networks with many layers (deep learning) are excellent for learning from large amounts of data and have significantly advanced fields like image recognition, natural language processing, and autonomous driving.

As shown in Table **4**, common supervised learning algorithms include Linear Regression, Logistic Regression, Decision Trees, Random Forest, K-Nearest Neighbors (K-NN), Support Vector Machines (SVM), Ensemble Methods, and Neural Networks. Linear Regression is used for forecasting and understanding variable importance by modeling the relationship between a continuous target variable and independent variables. Logistic Regression is suitable for binary classification tasks, modeling the probability of outcomes like 'success' or 'failure'. Decision Trees are a non-parametric method that learns simple decision rules from data features, while Random Forest improves accuracy by combining multiple decision trees to reduce overfitting. K-NN is an instance-based learning method that predicts labels based on the nearest K training examples. SVMs function by finding a hyperplane to separate different classes, making them effective for both linear and non-linear classification. Ensemble Methods improve prediction accuracy by combining multiple models, and Neural Networks are used for pattern recognition and sensory data interpretation, commonly applied in fields like image recognition and natural language processing.

Table 4. Common supervised learning algorithms.

Algorithm Name	Type	Description
Linear Regression	Regression	Models the relationship between a dependent continuous target variable and one or more independent variables, often used for forecasting and understanding variable importance.
Logistic Regression	Classification	Used for binary classification tasks, modeling the probability of the default class (*e.g.*, 'success' or 'failure'), suitable for dichotomous or binary outcomes.
Decision Trees	Classification and Regression	Non-parametric method that learns to make decisions based on simple decision rules inferred from the data features.
Random Forest	Classification and Regression	Improves prediction accuracy by building multiple decision trees and merging their outputs to control overfitting and enhance model robustness.
K-Nearest Neighbors (K-NN)	Classification and Regression	An instance-based learning method where the model predicts labels based on the nearest K training examples in the feature space.
Support Vector Machines (SVM)	Classification and Regression	Effective for both linear and non-linear classification, SVMs function by finding a hyperplane in a high-dimensional space to separate different classes.
Ensemble Methods	Classification and Regression	Techniques like bagging and boosting that combine multiple models to improve prediction accuracy and robustness.
Neural Networks	Classification and Regression	Algorithms designed to recognize patterns and interpret sensory data are significantly used in image recognition, natural language processing, and autonomous systems.

Evaluation Metrics

The performance of supervised learning models is often evaluated using various metrics. These metrics help us understand how well our model is doing, and they can guide us during the model selection and tuning stages. Here are some commonly used metrics:

Accuracy: While it is the most straightforward measure, accuracy can sometimes be misleading, especially in cases of imbalanced datasets where the majority class dominates the prediction. In such cases, even a naive model that always predicts the majority class can achieve a high accuracy score.

Precision: This metric is particularly useful in scenarios where the consequence of a false positive is significant. For example, in spam detection, a false positive (non-spam email classified as spam) could mean missing an important email, hence precision is crucial.

Recall (Sensitivity): Recall becomes a critical measure when the cost of missing a true positive is high. For instance, in medical diagnostics for a serious disease, it is vital to capture as many true cases as possible, making recall extremely important.

F1 Score: The F1 score is useful in situations with uneven class distributions or when one cares equally about precision and recall. It is particularly beneficial in situations where both false positives and false negatives carry a high cost, such as in document classification or legal proceedings.

Precision-Recall Curve: This curve helps in identifying the trade-off between precision and recall for different probability thresholds. A higher area under the curve represents both high recall and high precision, where high precision relates to a low false positive rate, and high recall relates to a low false negative rate.

ROC Curve: The ROC (Receiver Operating Characteristics) curve is effective for visualizing the trade-off between the true positive rate and false positive rate across various thresholds. It is widely used in binary classification to determine the optimal model threshold for separating classes.

AUC (Area Under Curve): AUC provides an aggregate measure of performance across all possible classification thresholds. One way of interpreting AUC is the probability that the model ranks a random positive example more highly than a random negative example.

As shown in Table **5**, various evaluation metrics are used to assess supervised learning models, including Accuracy, Precision, Recall, F1 Score, ROC Curve, and AUC (Area Under Curve). Accuracy is simple and intuitive, measuring the proportion of correct predictions made by the model, but it can be misleading in unbalanced datasets. Precision focuses on avoiding false positives, making it useful when the cost of false positives is high, such as in spam filtering. Recall emphasizes avoiding false negatives, which is critical in scenarios like disease screening. The F1 Score balances precision and recall, making it ideal when both metrics are equally important. The ROC Curve provides a comprehensive view of the threshold effects, while AUC offers a single measure of model performance, which is useful for comparing models or configurations but does not reflect class distribution or cost-sensitivity.

Table 5. Supervised learning evaluation metrics.

Metric Name	Description	Advantages	Disadvantages	Applicable Scenarios
Accuracy	The proportion of correct predictions made by the model.	Simple and intuitive.	Can be misleading in unbalanced datasets.	Suitable when data categories are balanced.
Precision	Proportion of actual positives among predicted positives.	Emphasizes avoiding false positives.	May overlook the number of false negatives.	Useful when the cost of false positives is high, such as in spam filtering.
Recall	The proportion of actual positives correctly predicted as positive.	Emphasizes avoiding false negatives.	May tolerate an increase in false positives.	Critical when the cost of false negatives is high, such as in disease screening.
F1 Score	The harmonic mean of precision and recall, a balance of both.	Balances precision and recall.	Not sensitive to extreme values.	When both precision and recall are important.
ROC Curve	Graph showing the relationship between true positive rate and false positive rate at various thresholds.	Provides a comprehensive view of threshold effects.	Requires graphical interpretation, and can be challenging to compare models numerically.	For evaluating overall classifier performance, especially with multiple classes or when adjusting decision thresholds.
AUC (Area Under Curve)	The area under the ROC curve measures overall model performance.	Provides a single measure of model performance.	Does not reflect class distribution or cost-sensitivity.	Useful for comparing models or multiple configurations.

For regression problems, other metrics are used:

Mean Squared Error (MSE): The average squared differences between predicted and actual outcomes. It is a popular metric but can disproportionately give higher weights to bigger errors.

Root Mean Squared Error (RMSE): RMSE is even more sensitive to outliers than MSE due to the squaring of prediction errors which emphasizes larger errors more so than smaller ones. It provides a measure of how large errors are spread out across the dataset.

Mean Absolute Error (MAE): Since MAE takes the absolute value of the error, it provides a linear score that does not square the error results. This makes it less sensitive to outliers compared to MSE or RMSE. MAE offers a more direct and interpretable measurement of average error magnitude.

All these metrics give us a different perspective on the performance of the model, and it is important to select the right metric based on the goal of our machine-learning model.

Application Examples

Certainly, supervised learning has found widespread applications in various fields for decision-making processes. Below are some real-world use cases across different industries:

Medical Diagnosis: Supervised learning algorithms, particularly logistic regression, and neural networks, play a pivotal role in the field of medical diagnostics. These algorithms are trained on historical health data including symptoms, diagnostics, and outcomes to predict patient diseases. For instance, neural networks have been effectively used to predict the likelihood of diabetes in patients based on input features like age, body mass index, insulin levels, and blood pressure. This approach not only enhances diagnostic accuracy but also aids in the early detection of diseases, which can be crucial for effective treatment.

Marketing Forecast: In marketing, supervised learning techniques such as linear regression and decision trees analyze historical sales data and other relevant indicators like seasonal trends, promotional campaigns, and consumer demographics to forecast future sales. This allows companies to optimize inventory management, adjust marketing strategies, and allocate resources more efficiently to meet anticipated demand. For example, a retail chain might use these models to predict holiday season sales and adjust its stock levels accordingly to maximize revenue.

Credit Scoring: Financial institutions rely on supervised learning to assess the creditworthiness of individuals. Methods like support vector machines (SVM) and random forests analyze past financial behavior and demographic information to predict credit risks. These models process inputs such as credit history length, repayment records, and outstanding debts to assign credit scores. This automated assessment helps banks and credit agencies decide whom to grant loans to and at what interest rates, effectively managing financial risk.

Image Recognition: Convolutional Neural Networks (CNNs) are a specialized kind of neural network used extensively in image recognition tasks. They are trained on large datasets of images to recognize patterns and classify images based on their content. For example, a CNN might be trained to differentiate between images of cats and dogs by recognizing distinct features such as shapes, sizes, and textures. This technology is fundamental in applications ranging from automated photo tagging in social media to advanced medical imaging techniques that help identify diseases from X-rays and MRI scans.

Speech Recognition: Speech recognition software utilizes supervised learning algorithms, including Hidden Markov Models (HMMs) and neural networks, to convert spoken language into text. These models are trained on a corpus of speech data and corresponding transcriptions. They learn to understand various accents, intonations, and speech nuances. Modern voice-activated assistants like Siri and Alexa rely on these technologies to interpret user commands and perform actions accordingly, making user interfaces more interactive and accessible.

Natural Language Processing (NLP): In NLP, supervised learning is used for tasks such as sentiment analysis, where algorithms classify text as expressing positive, negative, or neutral sentiments. Techniques such as Naive Bayes, decision trees, or Recurrent Neural Networks (RNNs) are trained on labeled datasets of text to learn how linguistic features correspond to sentiment. This application is particularly valuable for businesses to monitor brand perception in social media or for financial analysts to gauge market sentiment from news articles and predict stock movements.

These examples illustrate the broad application of supervised learning algorithms in addressing real-world problems. They can be applied to any task involving data prediction or classification, making them an invaluable tool in many industries.

Looking forward, the field of supervised learning offers several promising areas for future research:

Deep Learning in Supervised Learning: While conventional supervised learning techniques have a set architecture, deep learning, a subset of machine learning, allows for models with higher complexity. This includes Convolutional Neural Networks (CNNs) for image recognition, Recurrent Neural Networks (RNNs) for sequence data, and Transformer models for NLP tasks. Exploring and improving these architectures for better performance and efficiency is a critical aspect of future research.

Adversarial Training Challenges: Adversarial training pertains to instances where small, intentionally crafted perturbations to the input lead to incorrect model output. Recent years have seen a surge in adversarial attacks on machine learning models, particularly in the field of image recognition. Understanding and mitigating these attacks is a key challenge that researchers are currently grappling with.

Explainability and Trust in AI: As machine learning models, especially deep learning ones, become increasingly complex, they also become more of a "black box, " making their outputs hard to interpret. Researching methods for increasing model explainability can help foster trust in AI systems and ensure their decisions can be understood and validated.

Fairness and Bias in Machine Learning: Machine learning models are only as good as the data they're trained on, and if the training data is biased, the model's predictions will also be biased. Future research will need to address these issues, developing methodologies for fair and unbiased machine learning.

Efficient Training Techniques: As data volume grows exponentially, training larger models efficiently becomes increasingly important. Future research could focus on investigating novel training methods, optimizing existing algorithms, or even developing hardware specifically designed for machine learning tasks.

In conclusion, supervised learning, as a traditional machine learning area, has a plethora of open-ended questions and potential research directions, fostering its continued relevance in the years to come.

The Enchanting Dance of the Catboost Algorithm

CatBoost is a high-performance, open-source gradient boosting library developed by Yandex, the Russian search engine giant. The name "CatBoost" in itself is an abbreviation for "Category" and "Boosting". It is an algorithm that specializes in working with categorical data and boosting, making it unique and adept for several applications.

In a world overflowing with data, much of it comes in the form of categorical variables. Effective handling of these categorical variables is what lends the CatBoost algorithm its unique strength. Unlike other models that require extensive preprocessing to handle categorical variables, CatBoost can use them directly, leading to significantly higher prediction accuracy.

Speaking of its applications, CatBoost can be used for a variety of tasks requiring predictive modeling with categorical data. Owing to its exceptional handling of categorical data, the CatBoost algorithm is highly effective in problems ranging from customer churn prediction, price prediction, and fraud detection, to medical diagnoses, and much more.

In summary, CatBoost is a powerful, flexible algorithm that provides excellent handling for categorical variables and strong predictive power, making it a leading tool in the field of machine learning.

CatBoost stands out for its handling of categorical features and the prevention of overfitting. Let us delve into these core principles:

Handling Categorical Features

Most machine learning algorithms require categorical variables to be converted into numerical form before they can be processed. However, these encoding methods can sometimes lead to a loss of information. CatBoost simplifies this by offering a more refined approach. It implements an encoding scheme that computes conditional statistics for categorical values before feeding them into the model. This process involves calculating various statistics (like mean) of the target variable conditioning on each categorical value, without leaking information from the test set, therefore providing a richer and more accurate representation of the categorical features.

Preventing Overfitting

Overfitting is a common problem where a machine learning model performs well on the training data but fails to generalize on unseen data. To tackle this, CatBoost uses a technique called Ordered Boosting. Unlike standard boosting algorithms that use the same data to build each tree in the sequence, CatBoost adjusts the data at each step by introducing a random permutation of the learning sample and computes the statistics for the encoding only on the objects before the processed one in the permutation. This 'ordered target statistic' approach dramatically reduces overfitting.

Also, CatBoost has a built-in mechanism to handle different types of overfitting by implementing a systemic search for hyperparameters. It constructs multiple alternatives using different sets of hyperparameters and chooses the one variant that delivers the best cross-validation.

In conclusion, the efficacy of CatBoost comes down to its unique approach to processing categorical features directly and efficiently, as well as its smart techniques to avoid overfitting, making it a reliable and robust algorithm for various predictive modeling tasks.

CatBoost has several powerful features that distinguish it from other gradient-boosting machines. Here are the primary characteristics:

Excellent Handling of Categorical Features: One of the main advantages of CatBoost is its ability to handle categorical features automatically. It uses a statistical technique to convert categorical features into numerical format, which eliminates the need for intensive pre-processing that can introduce errors. It addresses the issue of categorical feature handling by calculating various statistics (like mean) of the target variable, conditioned on each categorical value.

Designed to Control Overfitting: One of the common problems in machine learning is overfitting where a model learns the detail and noise in the training data and performs poorly on unseen data. CatBoost uses ordered boosting, an iterative and sequential algorithm, which allows it to successfully manage the overfitting problem and ensure accurate and reliable model predictions.

Superior Accuracy: CatBoost delivers a more accurate performance compared to other gradient-boosting algorithms. With its uniquely efficient handling of categorical inputs, CatBoost often outperforms other models when a dataset has many categorical features. Incorporating an ordered target statistic approach has been shown to provide better performance, especially on datasets with categorical features.

GPU Training: In addition to being efficient, CatBoost is also designed to be fast. It allows you to utilize the full power of your GPU, massively reducing the time needed to train models without sacrificing accuracy.

User-Friendly: CatBoost also comes with several user-friendly features like built-in handling of missing values and automatic parameter tuning, which can save a lot of time during model development. Additionally, CatBoost can be easily integrated with Python and R environments, making it extremely user-friendly.

In conclusion, CatBoost offers a powerful, efficient, and convenient method for building gradient-boosting models, especially in scenarios with lots of categorical features. Its effort to manage overfitting and the simplicity of use pads up its position in the machine learning toolbox.

CatBoost, XGBoost, and LightGBM are popular gradient-boosting libraries widely used for classification and regression tasks. However, they differ in their ability to handle category features and resist overfitting.

- **Processing Category Features:** Most machine learning algorithms require preprocessing when processing category features, such as single hot encoding or label encoding. However, CatBoost can directly handle category features. It uses a special encoding scheme to process category features, which can achieve good results without the need for additional steps. However, other libraries such as XGBoost and LightGBM may require users to preprocess category features themselves.

- **Prevent Overfitting:** CatBoost uses a method called "Ordered Boosting" to prevent overfitting, which adjusts the data at each step. However, although XGBoost and LightGBM also provide some parameters to prevent overfitting, they may not be as resistant to overfitting as CatBoost by default.
- **Performance and Speed:** CatBoost performs excellently in accuracy and running speed in many standard benchmark tests. Especially, due to its efficient processing of category features, CatBoost often performs well on datasets containing a large number of category features.

Overall, although XGBoost and LightGBM perform well in many tasks, CatBoost's ability to handle category features and its built-in ability to prevent overfitting give it an advantage in dealing with more complex and diverse category features.

To install CatBoost, you can utilize pip or conda, which are package managers for Python.

Installing with pip

The command is quite straightforward. All you need is to open your command line and key in:

plaintext

pip install catboost

Installing with Conda

If you are using the Anaconda Python distribution, you can use the conda command for CatBoost installation. Open your command line and key in:

plaintext

conda install -c conda-forge catboost

Once installed, you can verify by importing the library into your python environment:

python

import catboost

If there's no error, it means CatBoost is successfully installed.

Now, let's see how we can use CatBoost on a simple regression problem:

Assume you have a house price prediction problem, and your data is already split into a training set and a test set (X_train, X_test, y_train, y_test).

python

```
from catboost import CatBoostRegressor

# initialize CatBoostRegressor

model = CatBoostRegressor(iterations=50, depth=3, learning_rate=0.1, loss_function='RMSE')

# fit the model with the training data

model.fit(X_train, y_train)

# make the prediction using the resulting model

preds = model.predict(X_test)
```

In this example, we first import CatBoostRegressor, then specify the parameters we want to use in our model like the number of iterations, tree depth, learning rate, and loss function to 'RMSE'. We fit the model using the 'fit' method, and generate the predictions with the 'predict' method.

Kindly refer to CatBoost's official documentation for more detailed information.

CatBoost has found its application in a wide array of fields. Here are a few examples:

- **Medical Diagnosis:** CatBoost has been used in predicting disease outcomes based on patient data. For example, in a study published in Frontiers in Genetics, researchers successfully utilized CatBoost to develop a predictive model for Type 2 Diabetes using genetic risk factors.
- **Financial Risk Control:** Financial institutions use CatBoost for fraud detection and credit scoring. CatBoost's handling of categorical variables, such as transaction types or credit history statuses, can boost the performance of these models.
- **Advertising:** Companies use CatBoost to predict ad click-through rates, which is essential in programmatic advertising. By utilizing user and ad variables, CatBoost can predict user behavior, improving ad targeting and bidding

strategies.

- **Recommendation Systems:** CatBoost is used in recommendation systems to predict user-item interactions. Yandex, the company behind CatBoost, uses it in its own recommendation systems.
- **Natural Language Processing (NLP):** CatBoost can also be applied to text classification problems. For example, CatBoost was used in the 'Toxic Comment Classification Challenge' on Kaggle to detect and classify toxic online comments.
- **Predictive Maintenance:** Companies use CatBoost to predict the failure or required maintenance of equipment based on sensor data and usage patterns. This can help prevent equipment failure and downtime.

These applications demonstrate CatBoost's adaptability to different types of data and its robustness in real-world predictive tasks, making it a valuable tool in many sectors.

While CatBoost is a robust and user-friendly library, users can still encounter several challenges when working with it. Here are a few potential issues and their solutions:

- **Data Preprocessing:** Although CatBoost handles categorical features directly, it doesn't mean you can ignore the data preprocessing step completely. Particularly, missing data still needs to be handled before fitting the model, as CatBoost does not support missing values. To handle missing data, you can use techniques like Imputation, where missing values are replaced with statistical measures such as mean, median, or mode.
- **Handling Text Features:** While CatBoost can handle categorical features efficiently, it does not directly handle text data or natural language features. For these, you might need to employ other techniques (like TF-IDF, Word2Vec) to convert text into a numerical representation before feeding it to CatBoost.
- **Parameter Tuning:** While CatBoost performs quite well with default parameters, there is potential for improvement with parameter tuning. The tuning of parameters often requires a lot of trials and can be time-consuming. Techniques such as Grid Search or Randomized Search can be used for hyperparameter tuning to search different combinations of parameters to find the best-performing ones.
- **Overfitting:** Even though CatBoost is designed to mitigate overfitting, when the model complexity is high due to too many features or very deep trees, overfitting can still occur. Regularization parameters in CatBoost can be adjusted to add penalties for complexity, thereby reducing overfitting.
- **Interpretability:** Like other boosting methods, CatBoost models can be hard to interpret. Using Shapley values or building Partial Dependence Plots can help

provide insights into the model's decision-making process.

By understanding these potential issues and their solutions, you can leverage CatBoost more effectively in your machine-learning projects.

Although CatBoost is a sophisticated machine learning algorithm, users can encounter a few challenges during its application. Here are some potential issues and their solutions:

- **Data Preprocessing:** While CatBoost's ability to directly handle categorical data without manual encoding provides a significant advantage, it does not inherently manage missing data, which can lead to issues during model training.

Expanded Solutions

Imputation: This involves filling missing values with substitute values based on statistical measures. Common techniques include:

Mean/Median Imputation: Replace missing values with the mean or median of the column, which is effective for numerical data not heavily skewed.

Mode Imputation: For categorical data, replacing missing values with the most frequent category can be effective.

Advanced Imputation Techniques: Using algorithms like k-Nearest Neighbors (k-NN) or multivariate imputation by chained equations (MICE) can provide a more sophisticated handling of missing data by considering the relationships between features.

- **Text Data:** CatBoost requires that all input data be numerical. Thus, text data must be appropriately converted before it can be used in training.

Expanded Solution

Vectorization: We convert text into numerical data using methods like TF-IDF, which transforms text into a vector that represents the frequency of terms adjusted for their relevance across multiple documents.

Embeddings: Pre-trained embeddings are used like Word2Vec or GloVe to convert words into dense vectors that capture semantic meanings. This can be particularly powerful for datasets with substantial textual data, providing a nuanced understanding of language patterns.

Feature Engineering: Through this feature, we can extract additional features from text such as sentiment scores, text length, or specific keyword flags that might be relevant for the prediction task.

- **Hyperparameter Tuning:** Finding the optimal settings for CatBoost parameters is crucial but can be resource-intensive and complex.

Expanded Solution

Automated Tools: Use tools like GridSearchCV or RandomizedSearchCV from the Scikit-learn library to systematically explore combinations of parameters. RandomizedSearchCV can be particularly effective by sampling a subset of parameter combinations, which reduces the computational cost.

Bayesian Optimization: Implement Bayesian optimization techniques which use prior probability distributions of the parameters to find the best parameters more efficiently than random or exhaustive searches.

Validation Curves: Plot validation curves to understand the relationship between each hyperparameter and the model's performance on the training and validation sets. This visual approach helps in identifying overfitting and underfitting scenarios.

- **Overfitting:** Despite built-in mechanisms to prevent overfitting, CatBoost can still overfit to noisy or overly complex training data.

Expanded Solution

Cross-Validation: K-fold cross-validation is used to ensure that the model generalizes well to unseen data. This technique also helps in understanding the stability of the model across different subsets of data.

Regularization: This increases the strength of L2 regularization (L2_leaf_reg parameter) to penalize large coefficients in the model, which typically reduces overfitting by simplifying the model.

Early Stopping: Early stopping is implemented to halt training once the performance on a held-out validation set stops improving, preventing unnecessary model complexity.

- **Black-Box Nature:** Like most machine learning models, CatBoost may act as a black box, creating an interpretability issue. Understanding the contributions of each feature can be a challenge. This can be mitigated by using methods such as SHAP (SHapley Additive exPlanations) to understand the output of the model.

Expanded Solution

SHAP Values: SHAP (SHapley Additive exPlanations) values are utilized to break down the output of the model into the contributions of each feature for individual predictions. This approach not only offers insights into the model's decision-making process but also helps in identifying potential biases in the model.

Feature Importance: We can regularly assess and review the feature importances generated by CatBoost, which can provide straightforward insights into which variables are driving the predictions.

Partial Dependence Plots: Use partial dependence plots to visualize the marginal effect of one or two features on the predicted outcome, offering a more intuitive understanding of the relationship between the features and the target.

In conclusion, while CatBoost offers flexibility and robustness, understanding possible challenges and their solutions will allow you to apply CatBoost effectively.

Becoming a Catboost Master: The Magic of Parameter Tuning

Parameter tuning, also known as hyperparameter optimization, is the process of selecting the set of optimal parameters for a machine learning model. The parameters, sometimes called hyperparameters, are the knobs of the model that are set before training begins. They govern the model's structure (*e.g.*, the depth of trees in Random Forest and CatBoost) or how it learns (*e.g.*, the learning rate in gradient boosting models).

Parameter tuning is crucial for several reasons. First, good parameters can help a model strike the right balance between bias and variance, essentially guiding how complex the model should be. Too simple, and the model might underfit, failing to find key patterns in the data. Too complex, and the model might overfit, falsely inferring noise in the data as patterns.

Secondly, well-tuned parameters can also make a model more efficient to train. For example, in gradient boosting algorithms like CatBoost, the learning rate, and the number of trees (iterations) can have a significant impact on training speed.

In our subsequent discussion, we'll delve deeper into the efficient and effective application of CatBoost focusing on how it can benefit from parameter tuning. We'll also touch on how to use different strategies for hyperparameter tuning and its effect on model performance. This discussion aims to provide a strong foundation for mastering parameter tuning in CatBoost, one of the most powerful machine learning algorithms in use today.

In CatBoost, there are several important parameters that you can adjust based on your dataset and problem:

Iterations: Also known as the number of trees. It defines the number of trees to be built in the model. The more trees you build, the more complex your model will be. While having a large number of trees can improve the accuracy of your model, it can also lead to overfitting if this parameter is set too high.

Depth: Represents the depth of the trees in the model. Deeper trees are more complex and can capture more information about the data. However, similar to the number of trees, a higher tree depth can cause overfitting.

Learning Rate: This is a very important parameter and it represents the speed at which the model learns. A smaller learning rate means the model will learn slowly and might need more trees to reach good performance. A larger learning rate will make the model learn faster, but may skip over optimal solutions.

Loss Function: The metric that the model will try to minimize. The choice of loss function depends on the kind of problem you are trying to solve. For binary classification, it could be 'Logloss', for regression it might be 'RMSE', and for multiclass problems, it might be 'MultiClass'.

L2_leaf_reg: A parameter that controls the L2 regularization on the weights. Increasing this value will make the model more conservative, and can prevent overfitting to an extent.

Border_count: This is the number of splits for numerical features. Higher values can potentially lead to improved accuracy but might slow down the training and prediction time.

These are some of the key parameters that can be tuned in CatBoost. It is pivotal to note that adjusting these parameters must be done carefully, as they can significantly impact the model's performance and training time. Therefore, understanding these parameters and knowing how to adjust them based on the characteristics of your data and the problem you're trying to solve is key to effectively using CatBoost.

Let's delve into the impact of key parameters like learning_rate, depth, and iterations on CatBoost's model performance, and how to properly choose these parameters across different scenarios.

Learning Rate: The learning rate controls the step size at each iteration while moving toward a minimum of a loss function. It profoundly impacts the speed and the quality of learning. A smaller learning rate requires more iterations but often results in better performance. Conversely, a larger learning rate leads to faster training but may not converge or might skip over the optimal solution. Hence, it is necessary to select a balanced learning rate after trying a few different values, typically between 0.01 and 0.3.

Depth: The Depth parameter in CatBoost controls the depth of trees in the model. A higher depth means more complex models, enabling the model to fit more complex patterns in the data. Still, it also increases the risk of overfitting. Conversely, a lower depth reduces complexity, making the model train faster and less prone to overfitting. The optimal depth, however, depends on the complexity and nature of the dataset.

Iterations: Iterations are the number of boosting steps to be performed, synonymous with the number of trees to build in the model. While having more iterations can lead to a more accurate model, having too many iterations can lead to overfitting and is also computationally expensive. A common practice is to start with a high learning rate with fewer trees, then decrease the learning rate while increasing the number of trees iteratively.

In different scenarios, these parameters should be adjusted accordingly. For instance, if the dataset is large and complex, a higher learning rate with more iterations and higher depth could lead to a better model. However, if the model is overfitting, reducing depth, lowering the learning rate, or reducing iterations could help. In any case, these parameters are typically tuned through techniques like grid search and cross-validation to obtain optimal values.

It is important to remember that these parameters interact significantly; changing one may require changes to others to maintain a well-performing model. Thus, parameter tuning often involves experimentation and iterative refinement.

Parameter tuning is a critical step in maximizing a model's performance. Here are the two most common strategies: Grid Search and Random Search.

- **Grid Search**: As the name suggests, Grid Search involves creating a 'grid' of hyperparameters and systematically trying out every possible combination. For example, if we're tuning 'depth' and 'learning_rate', and we decide to try out five different values for each, we will end up training 5*5=25 different models with all combinations. The combination that performs best (for instance, that yields the highest accuracy or lowest loss) is then chosen as the optimal hyperparameter.

The advantage of Grid Search is that it is exhaustive - we try out every possible combination of parameters, so we are likely to find the best one. However, it can be very time-consuming, especially if you have many parameters or if each model takes a long time to train.

- **Random Search**: Instead of trying out every possible combination, Random Search involves selecting a random value for each hyperparameter at each iteration. We decide beforehand how many iterations we want to do, unlike Grid Search, where this is determined by the number of combinations.

Random Search works on the belief that the best parameters are likely to be found in a random selection, given a sufficient number of iterations. It is a lot more time-efficient than Grid Search since we do not have to try out every possible parameter combination. However, it may miss the absolute optimal values since it is not an exhaustive search.

In practice, both methods can be used with CatBoost, depending on the size of your dataset, time constraints, and how many resources you have available. You typically start with a coarse grid or random search to find a good area, and then use a finer grid search in that specific area.

Both grid search and random search along with cross-validation implementation are supported in the Scikit-Learn library, which can be utilized with CatBoost models.

Let us consider a binary classification problem like predicting whether a customer will churn (*i.e.*, leave the company) or not based on different customer characteristics. We will not go deep into the feature engineering steps but directly into the parameter tuning of the CatBoost model for this problem.

First, let us assume you have already split your data into training and test sets and your CatBoost classifier is ready to go with default parameters:

```
python

from catboost import CatBoostClassifier

# define model with default parameters

model = CatBoostClassifier(random_seed=42, verbose=False)

# fit the model

model.fit(X_train, y_train)
```

Testing this base model on your validation set, let us say you get an accuracy of 85%. But you believe that it can be improved by tuning the parameters.

You decide to tune three parameters: iterations, learning_rate, and depth.

python

```
from sklearn.model_selection import GridSearchCV

# define parameter grid

param_grid = {'iterations': [100, 250, 500],

'learning_rate': [0.03, 0.1, 0.2],

'depth': [4, 6, 10]}

grid = GridSearchCV(estimator=CatBoostClassifier(random_seed=42, verbose= False),

param_grid = param_grid,

cv = 3,

scoring=”accuracy”)

# fit the model and search

grid.fit(X_train, y_train)

print(“Best Parameters: “, grid.best_params_)
```

Assuming that GridSearchCV found that the best parameters were 500 iterations, a learning rate of 0.1, and a depth of 6.

You can then create a new model with these parameters and likely find that performance is improved over the default parameters.

python

```
# define model with optimized parameters

optimized_model = CatBoostClassifier(iterations=500, learning_rate=0.1, depth=6, random_seed=42, verbose=False)

# fit the model
```

optimized_model.fit(X_train, y_train)

By using this approach, you might find that the accuracy of the predictions made by the model on the validation set improves to 89%. As shown in Fig. (**2**), the accuracy increases from 85% to 89% after optimizing the iterations, learning rate, and depth parameters, clearly demonstrating the effectiveness of the tuning process.

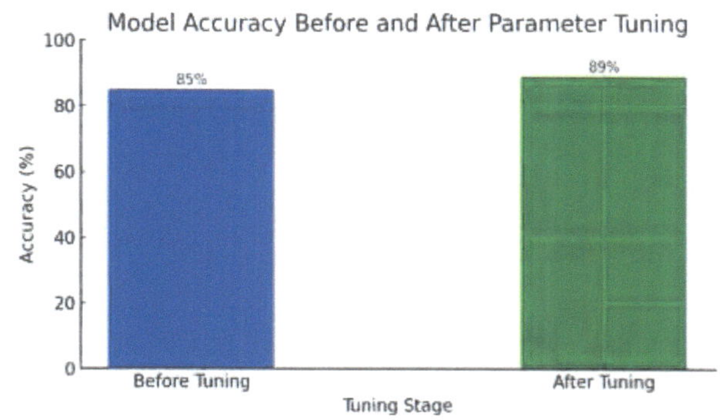

Fig. (2). Model accuracy before and after parameter tuning.

Remember, parameter tuning is a process that depends heavily on the specific dataset and the problem you're trying to solve. Different issues may require different strategies. The goal is to find the best parameters that make your model perform better on unseen data.

In machine learning, overfitting occurs when your model is too complex: it learns both existing patterns in data and noise. As a result, while the model may perform impressively on your training data, it performs poorly on unseen data. Although CatBoost is designed to automatically combat overfitting, there are several steps you can take to further mitigate this issue:

- **Limit Tree Depth**: By decreasing the depth parameter, you decrease the complexity of the model. A lower tree depth may help prevent the model from learning the noise in the training data, making it more generalizable for unseen data.
- **Increase Regularization**: Regularization aims to prevent overfitting by adding a penalty for complexity to the model's loss function. In CatBoost, l2_leaf_reg is the key parameter for L2 regularization. An increasing l2_leaf_reg value makes the model more conservative.
- **Change Learning Rate and Iterations**: Another way to control overfitting in CatBoost is to adjust the learning_rate and iteration parameters together. A lower learning rate and higher number of iterations will cause the model to learn slower and potentially avoid overfitting—to a degree.

- **Use Early Stopping**: CatBoost also allows for early stopping wherein training stops automatically if the model's performance on a validation dataset has not improved for a given number of iterations. This can be controlled using the parameters early_stopping_rounds.
- **Cross-validation**: Apply cross-validation during model training which divides the dataset into training and validation folds. This gives a more honest assessment of a model's prediction power and aids in controlling overfitting.

By understanding these parameters and adjusting them accordingly, you can make a CatBoost model that is less prone to overfit and more capable of performing well on unseen data.

Cross-validation coupled with hyperparameter tuning is indeed a powerful approach to building more robust and high-performing models.

Cross-validation is a technique where the dataset is randomly split into 'k' groups or folds. After the split, each fold is used once as a validation set while the remaining k-1 groups form a training set. The performance measure is then averaged over the 'k' folds. This approach gives a more robust estimate of the model's performance on unseen data.

Here's how we can use cross-validation with CatBoost's parameters:

- **Manual Cross-Validation:** CatBoost provides the cv function that we can use to apply K-Fold cross-validation:

```
python

from catboost import cv, Pool

# define data pool

pool = Pool(X, y, cat_features=categorical_features_indices)

# specify parameters

params = {'iterations': 100,

'depth': 5,

'loss_function': 'Logloss',

'verbose': False}

# conduct cross-validation
```

scores = cv(pool, params, fold_count=5)

print cross-validation scoresprint(scores)

The cv function returns a DataFrame with cross-validation scores for each iteration.

- **Grid Search with Cross-Validation:** This approach allows us to perform hyperparameter tuning with cross-validation. Here's how we can use GridSearchCV from sci-kit-learn with CatBoost:

python

from sklearn.model_selection import GridSearchCVfrom catboost import CatBoostClassifier

define model

model = CatBoostClassifier(random_seed=42, verbose=False)

define parameter grid

param_grid = {'iterations': [100, 200],

'learning_rate': [0.1, 0.3],

'depth': [4, 6]}

setup grid search with cross-validation

grid = GridSearchCV(estimator=model, param_grid=param_grid, cv=5, scoring= ”accuracy”)

conduct grid search

grid.fit(X, y)

print(“Best Parameters: “, grid.best_params_)print(“Best Score: “, grid.best_score_)

This will return the best parameters from the specified grid, as well as the cross-validated score for the best parameter combination.

By using these approaches, you'll be able to conduct hyperparameter tuning with cross-validation and obtain more robust, accurate models.

Our exploration of CatBoost's hyperparameters definitely does not have to stop here. As we keep pushing for better and more efficient models, some directions we can explore in the future could include:

- **Advanced Hyperparameter Optimization Techniques:** Apart from Grid Search and Random Search, other hyperparameter optimization strategies are gaining popularity. One notable method is Bayesian Optimization. It is a sequential design strategy for global optimization of black-box functions that consider past evaluation results to choose the next values to evaluate. It can find better hyperparameters in fewer steps, making the optimization process more efficient.
- **Feature Selection:** Incorporating feature selection in the hyperparameter tuning process could lead to much more efficient models. It could also provide better generalization by reducing overfitting and improving the model's interpretability.
- **Automated Machine Learning (AutoML) Frameworks:** Techniques and tools that automatically select the best algorithm and hyperparameters for a task can also be used. With Google's AutoML, H2O's AutoML and TPOT, we can find a good set of parameters and algorithms quicker with lesser programming.
- **Explore More CatBoost Features:** CatBoost provides more features such as categorical feature statistics and combinations, support for various forms of categorical features, supervised and unsupervised embeddings, *etc.* for better predictions. Exploring them would draw us closer to harnessing the full power of CatBoost.
- **Multi-objective Hyperparameter Optimization**: This refers to tuning hyperparameters for more than one metric. For instance, tuning CatBoost for both high performance and low prediction time could be particularly useful.

The field of machine learning and AI is continually evolving, and newer strategies and techniques are being developed regularly. Staying updated with the latest advancements and continually incorporating them into our models is the way to better predictions and insights.

CONCLUSION

In conclusion, this chapter has underscored CatBoost's advantages, such as its ease of use and robustness against overfitting, which make it a powerful tool for data scientists. Its effectiveness in handling categorical data and delivering strong performance across various predictive tasks establishes it as a preferred choice in the arsenal of machine learning tools.

While CatBoost exhibits these strengths, it also faces certain limitations that necessitate future research. These include its computational intensity when dealing with large datasets and the need for additional preprocessing for non-numerical data types. Future research directions could focus on enhancing computational efficiency, expanding capabilities to handle unstructured data, and further advancing techniques to prevent overfitting. Exploring these areas will help leverage CatBoost's strengths more fully and mitigate its limitations, promising exciting advancements in predictive modeling.

REFERENCES

Ahmed, Z., Mohamed, K., Zeeshan, S., Dong, X. (2020). Artificial intelligence with multi-functional machine learning platform development for better healthcare and precision medicine. *Database (Oxford), 2020*, baaa010.
[http://dx.doi.org/10.1093/database/baaa010] [PMID: 32185396]

Gudivada, V., Apon, A., Ding, J. (2017). Data quality considerations for big data and machine learning: Going beyond data cleaning and transformations. *International Journal on Advances in Software, 10*(1), 1-20.

Tatineni, S., Boppana, V.R. (2021). AI-Powered devops and mlops frameworks: Enhancing collaboration, automation, and scalability in machine learning pipelines. *Journal of Artificial Intelligence Research and Applications, 1*(2), 58-88.

Zhu, J., Ge, Z., Song, Z., Gao, F. (2018). Review and big data perspectives on robust data mining approaches for industrial process modeling with outliers and missing data. *Annu. Rev. Contr., 46*, 107-133.
[http://dx.doi.org/10.1016/j.arcontrol.2018.09.003]

CHAPTER 3

Big Data in Market Forecasting

Abstract: Chapter 3 explores the pivotal role of Big Data in enhancing market forecasting. It delves into various aspects of Big Data, including its types, management techniques, and the indispensable tools like Hadoop and Spark that facilitate efficient data processing. Additionally, the chapter examines the application of analytics to Big Data and discusses real-world case studies to illustrate the transformative impact of Big Data across different industries.

Keywords: Big data, Case studies, Data analytics, Data management, Hadoop, Market forecasting, Predictive analytics, Spark.

INTRODUCTION

This chapter introduces the expansive realm of Big Data, defining its scope and significance in contemporary market forecasting. It discusses the various forms of data—structured, semi-structured, and unstructured—and the unique challenges they present. The chapter sets the stage for a comprehensive exploration of how Big Data is harnessed to extract meaningful insights that drive decision-making and forecasting in business and finance. Throughout history, researchers have explored various methods to manage and analyze these types of data. Notably, prior studies have emphasized the potential of Big Data to revolutionize decision-making processes by providing a more granular understanding of consumer behaviors and market trends (Acharya *et al.*, 2018; Janssen *et al.*, 2017; Sarker, 2021; Wang *et al.*, 2016).

Building on this foundation, our study contributes to the existing body of knowledge by exploring innovative techniques for integrating Big Data analytics into market forecasting. While previous research has primarily focused on the use of Big Data within specific sectors like healthcare or retail, this chapter broadens the scope, investigating its application across a diverse range of industries. Additionally, we introduce novel methodologies for handling the velocity and variety of Big Data, addressing the challenges of data veracity and value extraction in a more comprehensive and systematic way than prior studies.

Heng Chen

This chapter sets the stage for a comprehensive exploration of how Big Data is harnessed to extract meaningful insights that drive decision-making and forecasting in business and finance. By leveraging advanced analytical techniques and cross-industry comparisons, we aim to provide a deeper understanding of Big Data's transformative potential and outline strategic approaches for its effective implementation in market forecasting.

Dance of Data: Foundations of Big Data Knowledge

Big Data refers to the vast volumes of structured and unstructured data that businesses encounter daily, which can be analyzed for insights into trends and behaviors. But it is not just the amount of data that is important, it's what organizations do with the data that matters. Big Data can be analyzed to reveal patterns, trends, and associations, specifically relating to human behavior and interactions.

The concept of Big Data revolves around the exponential growth, availability, and use of information, both structured and unstructured. The main allure of Big Data is due to the sheer volume of information and data that is available for us to explore and harness to make better decisions in all aspects of society.

This brings us to the term “Dance of Data”. Comparing the world of Big Data to a dance represents the rhythm, the movement, and the patterns that we are trying to find within this vast amount of information. It is an intricate, ongoing process - we collect data, clean and process it, analyze and visualize it. If done right, the final product, much like a beautifully choreographed dance, is a smooth, comprehensive understanding of the patterns the data contains.

In this document, we are going to delve deeper and explore various aspects of Big Data. Here are some of the areas we will be touching:

- Understanding Big Data.
- Techniques for managing and processing Big Data.
- The role of Hadoop and Spark in handling Big Data.
- Applying analytics to Big Data.
- Case studies showing the application of Big Data in real-world scenarios.
- Upcoming trends in Big Data.
- Summarizing and drawing parallels to the 'Dance of Data'.

This document will serve as a foundation for understanding the intricate dance of Big Data and how to navigate this dance floor effectively.

Understanding Big DataGo deeper into what Big Data is

Big Data is a term that encapsulates data too large or complex to be dealt with by traditional data-processing methods. The term "Big Data" primarily refers to the vast amount of data that inundates businesses on a daily basis. It can be classified into three types:

- **Structured Data:** It refers to the data that can be stored, accessed, and processed in a fixed format. It tends to reside in relational databases (RDBMS).
- **Semi-Structured Data:** As the name suggests, it is a form of structured data that does not adhere to the formal structure of data models typically associated with relational databases.
- **Unstructured Data:** It is the data that does not possess a pre-defined model or is not organized in a predefined manner.

The secret to harnessing the potential of Big Data lies in capturing, storing, and analyzing this data to bring useful insights and make informed decisions.

When dealing with Big Data, we often refer to the 5Vs defining the challenges associated with it:

- **Volume:** The amount of data that's being stored and managed.
- **Velocity:** The speed at which new data is generated and rotated .
- **Variety:** The increasing types of data available, from structured data to semi-structured, and unstructured.
- **Veracity:** The quality and credibility of the data can vary greatly, affecting the accurate analysis.
- **Value:** The usefulness of the data being stored, and the insights derived from it, reflect its value.

Knowing how to work with Big Data—understanding its nuances, tackling its challenges, and leveraging it effectively—is crucial in numerous sectors today. From financial projections to customer interaction tracking, the usage and importance of Big Data are immense.

Key Techniques in Managing Big Data

Techniques for managing Big Data primarily focus on effective ways to process, store, and analyze large volumes of data. Two of the most common data processing techniques used are Batch Processing and Stream Processing.

Batch Processing is a technique for handling large chunks of data. Data is collected over a specified window of time and then processed as a single batch. This method is suitable when dealing with massive amounts of data that are not time-sensitive, such as calculating monthly reports or generating recommendations based on a user's past behavior. With batch processing, the complete data is available, providing a comprehensive view for analysis.

Stream Processing, on the other hand, is about analyzing and acting on real-time data. Unlike batch processing, it does not wait for data collection to complete. Instead, it processes each data item individually in real-time as it arrives. Stream processing is particularly valuable when decisions need to be made immediately, like fraud detection in banking transactions or real-time analytics in traffic management systems.

Alongside these data processing techniques, certain Machine Learning algorithms are more suited for Big Data due to their ability to handle large volumes of data efficiently:

Linear Regression and Logistic Regression are simple yet powerful algorithms that can work well with large datasets for predicting continuous outcomes or making binary classifications respectively.

Decision Trees and Random Forests are also preferred when dealing with Big Data due to their ease of implementation, interpretability, and ability to handle both numerical and categorical variables.

Gradient Boosting Algorithms such as XGBoost and CatBoost are known for their superior performance and speed, making them suitable for Big Data scenarios.

Deep Learning algorithms, especially those utilizing artificial neural networks, have shown remarkable results in Big Data. They excel at extracting patterns from unstructured data like images, audio, and text.

However, it is important to note that choosing an algorithm depends on the specific characteristics of your dataset and the problem you are trying to solve. While these techniques offer a starting point, a key part of managing Big Data is ongoing experimentation and adaptation as more data is collected.

Role of Hadoop and Spark in Big Data

Hadoop and Spark are both frameworks that are widely used for processing Big Data, each with its own set of capabilities and advantages.

Apache Hadoop is an open-source framework that allows distributed processing of large datasets across clusters of computers using simple programming models. It is designed to scale up from single servers to thousands of machines where each machine offers local computation and storage. Hadoop's main components are:

Hadoop Distributed File System (HDFS): This is where data is stored across multiple machines without any prior organization. It divides big data into smaller blocks, distributes them across nodes in a cluster, and reliably manages this data even in the event of hardware failure.

MapReduce: This is the programming model used by Hadoop for processing the data. The Map function takes a set of data and converts it into key/value pairs. The Reduce function then takes these pairs and reduces unrelated ones down to a single answer.

Apache Spark, on the other hand, is an open-source, distributed computing system. It provides an interface for programming clusters with implicit data parallelism and fault tolerance. Some key components of Spark are:

Resilient Distributed Datasets (RDDs): These are data structures - essentially an immutable distributed collection of objects. RDDs are split into multiple partitions, and they are automatically rebuilt on machine failure.

Spark Streaming: This component enables the processing of live data streams.

MLlib: This is Spark's scalable machine learning library.

GraphX: Spark's API for graph processing.

The main advantage of Spark over Hadoop lies in speed. Spark uses in-memory processing, meaning it keeps most of its data in RAM, allowing it faster access, and hence, it is significantly faster than Hadoop in iterative computations. However, due to its in-memory nature, Spark may be less suitable for extremely large datasets that do not fit into memory.

Both Apache Hadoop and Apache Spark play a critical role in the world of Big Data. They help in storing, processing, and analyzing large datasets efficiently. However, while they offer similar functionalities, their approach to doing so and their capabilities vary, making them suited to different types of Big Data tasks.

Data Analytics

Data analytics is the process of examining, cleaning, transforming, and modeling data to discover useful information, draw conclusions, and support decision-making. In the context of Big Data, analytics is applied to handle and analyze massive volumes of data that traditional software cannot manage. Here are the three key types of Big Data analytics:

- **Descriptive Analytics** is the simplest and most common method of data analysis. It answers the question, "What has happened?" by providing a historical view of the data. This form of analytics involves gathering data from multiple sources to give a comprehensive overview of past trends and patterns. For example, a retail business might use descriptive analytics to understand the total sales and average sales per region over the past year.
- **Predictive Analytics** goes a step further and uses historical data to predict future outcomes. It answers the question, "What could happen?" by using statistical models and forecasting techniques. For instance, an insurance company might use predictive analytics to forecast the probability of a claim being fraudulent based on past data and trends.
- **Prescriptive Analytics** speaks to possible actions and their likely outcomes to answer the question, "What should we do?" It uses complex algorithms and computational models to suggest the best course of action for a given scenario. For instance, a delivery company could use prescriptive analytics to optimize routes and delivery schedules to reduce costs and improve efficiency.

Big Data analytics tools make it possible to manage and analyze vast amounts of data, enabling companies to provide better customer service, create more targeted marketing strategies, and improve operational efficiency among other benefits. Understanding the differences between these types of analytics and knowing how and when to use them is crucial when dealing with Big Data.

Case Study: Big Data in Real World Scenarios

Big Data has found diverse applications across numerous industries, providing insights that drive critical decisions. Let's look into a few case studies to understand its impact:

Healthcare - Improving Patient Care

Predictive analytics and machine learning powered by Big Data are being used for early disease detection. For instance, Tempus, a technology company, is using Big Data to fight cancer. They analyze clinical and molecular data in real time to help doctors make more personalized treatment decisions for patients.

Business - Enhancing Customer Experience

Netflix, a prominent player in the entertainment industry, uses Big Data to understand user preferences and viewing patterns. This analysis fuels their recommendation engine, enabling Netflix to provide personalized content suggestions, improving user experience and retention.

Academics - Advancing Research

In academia, Big Data is being used to enhance research across various disciplines. For example, Harvard's Center for Geographic Analysis utilizes Big Data to tackle problems in different areas like health, elections, urban planning, and environmental changes. Through location tracking, they've been able to map disease spread and plan for effective health interventions.

Agriculture - Maximizing Crop Yields

Farmers and agricultural companies use Big Data analytics for precision farming. They use predictive analytics to optimize irrigation, find the right planting and harvesting times, and predict possible pest attacks—all through the analysis of weather data, soil data, crop data, and more. A case in point is John Deere, the iconic farming machinery manufacturer, embedding sensors into their machines to collect data that helps farmers make better decisions.

Sports - Improving Performance

Sports teams are using data analysis to enhance team performance. For example, the German national soccer team partnered with SAP during the World Cup 2014. They developed an application to collect and analyze performance data from training sessions, helping the coaches plan strategies and make vital game-time decisions.

These examples offer just a glimpse into the myriad possibilities presented by Big Data across different sectors. The insights derived from analyzing Big Data are helping industries to revolutionize their fields, paving the way for innovative methods to solve complex issues.

Future Trends in Big Data

As businesses continue to generate enormous amounts of data daily, technologies to handle, process, and gain insights from this data are continually evolving. Here are some of the trends we're seeing in Big Data:

- **Automated Machine Learning (AutoML):** Automation in machine learning can make it significantly more efficient and accessible. AutoML includes automating data pre-processing, feature selection, model selection, hyperparameter tuning, and analysis of results. This allows data scientists to scale their operations and build more models tailored to their needs.
- **Edge Computing:** With the rise of Internet of Things (IoT) devices, data is being generated at the edge of the network (*i.e.*, near data sources like sensors

and smartphones). Processing data right where it is generated reduces the latency, thereby enabling real-time insights and actions.

- **Quantum Computing:** Quantum Computers, once fully realized, could revolutionize data processing and machine learning. They hold the potential to quickly solve complex computational problems that are currently hard or impossible to solve—even with the most powerful supercomputers.
- **Integration of AI and Big Data:** Machine Learning and AI technologies are increasingly being used to analyze Big Data. As AI gets more integrated with Big Data, we can expect even more advanced analytics tools and techniques.
- **Enhanced Data Privacy and Security:** With Big Data growing larger every day, data privacy and security become crucial. We can expect to see more sophisticated methods of ensuring data privacy and increased regulations around data use.
- **DataOps:** Just as DevOps revolutionized software development, DataOps promises to boost the efficiency of data analytics pipelines. DataOps involves automating various phases of data analytics, from collection to processing to visualization.

Each of these trends shows promising potential in handling and harnessing Big Data, and its integration with other technology trends will likely result in even more profound impacts across different industries.

Conclusion & the Dancing Data

In conclusion, the concept of Big Data is a powerful force driving business strategies, academic research, tech innovations, and more. This "Dance of Data" - the collection, organization, and interpretation of vast amounts of information - is an intricate process that, when executed well, leads to valuable insights and business decisions.

In our exploration of Big Data, we began by understanding its essential elements, such as volume, variety, velocity, veracity, and value. We also discussed the different types of Big Data: structured, semi-structured, and unstructured - each with its unique rhythm and requiring specific moves to handle effectively.

The choreography of our dance included the crucial role of data processing techniques, where we gain efficiency and speed *via* methods like Batch Processing and Stream Processing. Advanced machine learning algorithms also came into play, each selected based on its unique benefits in handling large data sets.

Major platforms like Hadoop and Spark, our dance stages, have been instrumental in storing, processing, and analyzing Big Data. They each offer unique capabilities in handling large volumes of data, helping us perform and shine on the dance floor.

In the world of gaming, where the execution of each move depends on timing, we appreciate different forms of data analytics - Descriptive Analytics, Predictive Analytics, and Prescriptive Analytics - each bringing different elements to our dance, shaping the past, present, and future actions.

We then took a glance at the audience - different industries where our dance of Big Data makes notable performances. We saw breakthroughs in healthcare, innovations in business, advancements in research, and optimization in agriculture and sports.

It evolves with Automated Machine Learning, Edge Computing, Quantum Computing, and deeper integration of AI - all offering new rhythms to our dance.

Indeed, the Dance of Data, much like any dance, requires practice, understanding, and skill. But when done right, the patterns and rhythms we find lead to a beautiful and insightful performance - a dance that truly embodies the spirit and potential of Big Data.

The Magic of Data Cleaning

Introduction to Data Cleaning

Data cleaning, also referred to as data cleansing or data scrubbing, is the process of identifying and correcting or removing errors and inaccuracies from data in datasets. It involves detecting and dealing with anomalies, inaccuracies, and inconsistencies in datasets to improve their quality.

The importance of data cleaning stems from the outcomes of the process. First, it enhances the accuracy of the dataset, consequently improving the accuracy of the predictive model. Second, it allows for more efficient data usage, saving on storage, and improving performance. Third, it prevents duplicated and erroneous data entry, reduces the risk of making costly errors, and improves decision-making.

Data cleaning is a critical, indispensable step in the data preparation process, essential for ensuring the quality and reliability of the data for analysis, and crucial before any significant data analysis or data processing can occur. Without it, you may be drawing conclusions from inaccurate or incomplete data, which can lead to misleading results and flawed business decisions. It's much like ensuring you have a clean, well-prepared canvas before starting a painting.

In the following pages, we'll delve into more detail about the issues usually found in raw data, the step-by-step process of data cleaning, and some of the commonly used tools and techniques. We'll also present a case study on the application of data cleaning in real-world scenarios and discuss common mistakes to avoid. Lastly, we'll explore the role of machine learning and AI in data cleaning, and wrap up by underscoring the 'magic' in revealing clear, insightful data after the cleaning process.

Issues in Raw Data

Here we will highlight common problems in raw data, including inconsistencies, duplicate entries, missing data, and incorrect values and explain how these issues can affect data analysis.

Raw data, also known as source data or atomic data, often comes with numerous issues that need to be addressed before meaningful data analysis can take place. Some common problems in raw data include:

- **Inconsistencies:** Inconsistent data can emerge from various sources. One example could be inconsistent formats in date and time fields, with some entries recorded in the "MM/DD/YYYY" format and others in "DD/MM/YYYY" format. Another common inconsistency is the use of different names or codes for the same category or entity.
- **Duplicate Entries:** These occur when the same record is included multiple times. Duplicates can distort analytical results, such as inflating the count or the mean of a dataset.
- **Missing Data:** Real-world datasets often contain missing values. They could occur due to various reasons, such as failure to collect data, errors during data entry or extraction, or even data deletion. Missing values complicate the data cleaning process since it might not always be clear why the data is missing and how it should be treated.
- **Incorrect Values:** These could be due to errors in data collection, data entry, or other processes. For example, a person's age recorded as 300 or a field labeled 'weight' containing the entry 'New York' is clearly incorrect.

When it comes to how these issues can affect data analysis, they can lead to:

Skewed analytics and unreliable results: For example, duplicated records can make an item appear more popular than it is, or an inconsistent category name can split data into multiple groups, which could understate the real value.

Invalid model training: A machine learning model trained on such data will, at best, give incorrect predictions, and at worst, it might fail to function.

Misinformed decisions: The ultimate purpose of data analysis is to provide meaningful insights that can guide decisions. If the data is flawed, so too will be the decisions based on it.

Addressing these issues is a key step to ensure the quality of data and validity of the analytical results derived from it. The process of focusing on these issues and resolving them is an essential part of the magic of data cleaning.

Tools and Techniques for Data Cleaning

There are several tools and methods that are widely used for data cleaning. Here's a brief introduction to a few of them:

- **Excel:** Microsoft Excel is a great starting point for data cleaning, especially for smaller datasets. Excel offers a wide array of functions that can be used to identify and rectify errors in data. For instance, the Find and Replace feature can correct misspelled words or inconsistencies, Conditional Formatting can easily highlight errors, and Remove Duplicates can delete duplicate records.
- **OpenRefine:** Previously known as Google Refine, OpenRefine is a powerful tool for working with messy data. It allows you to clean and transform data across several rows simultaneously. One of its most powerful features is its clustering algorithms, which help to identify and correct inconsistent data entries.
- **Python Libraries:** Python, a popular programming language for data analysis, provides several libraries for efficient data cleaning:

Pandas: This library offers powerful data structures for data cleaning. You can use it to handle missing data, detect duplicate data, and change data types, among other tasks.

NumPy: Useful for numerical data, NumPy can replace missing values, remove outliers, and perform a host of other operations on number arrays.

Scikit-learn: This machine learning library provides several tools for data preprocessing, such as rescaling and normalization, dealing with categorical variables, and handling missing values.

- **SQL:** SQL (Structured Query Language) is also commonly used for data cleaning. By writing specific queries, you can identify anomalies, enforce integrity constraints, and delete or modify entries as needed.
- **Data Cleaning Services & Platforms:** For larger and more complex datasets, there are several data cleaning services and platforms available, like IBM's InfoSphere Information Server and Oracle's Enterprise Data Quality, which offer

robust tools to automate, simplify, and manage the data cleaning process on a large scale.

Each tool and method has its strengths and is best suited for specific types of data and specific situations. The choice of which to use often depends on the nature and size of the dataset, the desired outcome, and the resources available.

Case Study: Data Cleaning in Real-World Scenarios

All right, let us talk about a real-world example from the e-commerce industry.

Zalando, Europe's leading online fashion platform, has relied heavily on data cleaning for effective user behavior analysis. In the world of online shopping, businesses collect massive volumes of data, including clicks, page views, time spent on pages, purchases, and even mouse movements. However, this data is typically messy, inconsistent, and filled with missing or outlier values.

For example, one issue Zalando faced was inconsistent information across different data-gathering sources. Some users might sign up *via* social media accounts, others directly on the website, and yet others through their mobile app. This led to inconsistencies in the recorded user data, such as differences in the casing of text, varying date-time formats, or non-standard country codes. Moreover, there were discrepancies in the data reported by different analytics providers.

To tackle these problems, Zalando used a mixture of automated scripts and manual checks to clean their data. The scripts were designed to standardize the data, and manual checks were used to validate the outcomes. They corrected inconsistencies, filled in missing values based on sensible business conventions, and identified and rectified duplicate entries and incorrect values.

Once the data was cleaned, Zalando could then reliably analyze user behavior to gain comprehensive insights into the customer journey and improve the shopping experience. Cleansed data led to more accurate segmentation, more personalized communication, and improved targeting.

This case shows, how effective data cleaning not only improves the accuracy of analytics outcomes but ultimately leads to better business decisions and increased customer satisfaction.

The Role of Machine Learning and AI in Data Cleaning

Data cleaning is a crucial but often time-consuming part of the data analysis process. With the advent of AI and machine learning, there's significant potential to automate many aspects of data cleaning, making the process more efficient and less prone to human error. Here are several ways AI and machine learning can contribute:

- **Missing Data Imputation:** Machine learning algorithms can predict and fill in missing values based on the relationships observed in the rest of the data. Techniques include simple methods like mean, median, or mode imputation, or more complex ones like k-nearest neighbors (KNN) and regression imputation.
- **Anomaly Detection:** AI can efficiently identify anomalies or outliers in the datasets. These can be due to data entry errors, measurement errors, or genuine anomalies. Machine learning methods like Isolation Forest, DBSCAN, or autoencoders can identify such outliers for further inspection.
- **Duplicate Detection:** AI algorithms can be used to detect and eliminate duplicate entries in a dataset. This is particularly useful in large datasets where manual detection becomes practically impossible.
- **Data Standardization:** AI can help with standardizing data to maintain consistency and remove discrepancies. For example, it can standardize dates in a uniform format or categorize text data to a common casing.
- **Data Transformation:** Machine Learning methods can apply transformations to the data, making it suitable for analysis or visualization. This includes scaling and normalization, or encoding categorical data.
- **Feature Selection:** Machine learning can identify the most informative features and remove redundant ones, improving model efficiency and performance.

An example of an AI-driven data-cleaning tool is Holoclean. It uses statistical learning and reasoning to impute missing values, identify outliers, and resolve inconsistencies in databases.

While automating data cleaning through AI and machine learning holds a lot of promise, it is important to remember that these techniques are not entirely fault-tolerant. Human supervision and intervention are still necessary to confirm the changes and interpretations made by AI.

Conclusion and the 'Magic'

To summarize, data cleaning or data cleansing is an essential part of the data analysis process that involves identifying and addressing errors, inaccuracies, and inconsistencies in raw data. This process becomes increasingly important as the volume of data continues to grow with advancements in technology.

The problems often encountered in raw data - inconsistencies, duplicate entries, missing data, and incorrect values, can greatly affect the outcomes of data analysis and lead to misleading results if they aren't resolved at the earliest.

Recognizing these issues and knowing how to deal with them is the first step in the magic of data cleaning.

Various tools and techniques, from simple solutions like Excel to more complex ones like Python libraries (Pandas, NumPy, Scikit-learn), and services like IBM's InfoSphere or SQL, cater to the diverse needs of data cleaning.

The real transformation occurs when we successfully clean the data - raw data becomes meaningful information, offering invaluable insights and trends. In the real world, effective data cleaning can significantly enhance the results of data analysis, paving the way for better decision-making and predictive outcomes, as demonstrated in our discussion about its usage at Zalando.

Moreover, advancements in AI and machine learning open promising avenues for automating data cleaning, making it more efficient, and less prone to human error.

In essence, data cleaning is much like finding the signal in the noise. It cleans up the raw, often messy reality of datasets, transforming them, revealing patterns, insights and trends - the 'magic' in the data that informs strategies, solutions, and advancements. Like a dance that emerges beautiful and insightful from careful choreography, such is the magic of well-cleaned data.

Stellar Insights: Data Analysis and Mining

Introduction to Data Analysis and Mining

Data analysis and data mining are two key aspects of data science that, while interconnected, serve different purposes and involve different processes.

Data Analysis is the process of inspecting, cleaning, transforming, and modeling data to discover useful information and derive conclusions. It involves applying statistical, analytical, and logical techniques to provide insights that can guide decision-making.

The data analysis process generally includes steps such as data collection, data cleaning, data exploration with descriptive statistics or visualization, statistical analysis or predictive modeling, interpretation of results and reporting, often with an explicitly stated hypothesis or purpose to guide the analysis.

Data Mining, on the other hand, is a step further into the realm of discovering patterns in large data sets involving methods at the intersection of machine learning, statistics, and database systems. Data mining isn't aimed at answering specific questions. Instead, it's about discovering new, often surprising insights in large datasets.

The goal of data mining is to extract patterns and knowledge from vast amounts of data, not the extraction of data itself. It involves techniques such as clustering (finding hidden group patterns), association (discovering relationships between variables), and classification (predicting categorical labels), among others.

Both data analysis and data mining play vital roles in the data-driven world of today.

Data analysis helps companies, researchers, and organizations make informed decisions, streamline operations, better understand their customers or target audience, and identify trends and opportunities.

Data mining takes this a step further by helping to predict trends, understand complex relationships within data, and develop business strategies accordingly. It helps to predict customer behavior, detect fraud, forecast resource usage, devise focused marketing strategies, and a plethora of other applications.

In an age where data is being generated at a rate faster than we can analyze, both data analysis and data mining are invaluable for businesses and organizations to gain actionable insights, make informed decisions, and remain competitive

The Process of Data Analysis

Data analysis is a crucial step in making sense of raw information. It allows us to uncover patterns, find answers, and draw conclusions from seemingly disparate data points. Here's a walk-through of the typical processes involved in data analysis:

- **Formulation of Questions:** This is the initial stage where you identify what you want to find out from your data, often in the form of research questions or hypotheses.
- **Data Collection:** Depending on the question, you may need to collect new data or use existing data. This could come from databases, spreadsheets, text files, APIs, websites, or other sources.
- **Data Cleaning:** This is the process of identifying and correcting or removing errors, redundancies, and inconsistencies in the dataset. It is a crucial step to ensure that your data is accurate, consistent, and ready for analysis.
- **Data Exploration and Preprocessing:** At this stage, you may need to normalize or standardize your data, deal with missing values or outliers, and convert data types as necessary. Exploratory data analysis techniques such as summary statistics and data visualization help to understand the data's structure, uncover trends, and identify areas for further analysis.

- **Data Analysis:** Depending on your goals, you may use a range of techniques from basic descriptive statistics (mean, median, mode, *etc.*) to complex machine learning models (regression, clustering, classification). The aim is to identify patterns, relationships, and differences that answer your original questions.
- **Interpretation of Results and Drawing Conclusions:** Every analysis should culminate in an interpretation of the results. This might involve statistical tests to confirm the validity of the findings.
- **Communication of Findings:** The outcomes of your analysis should be presented in an accessible and understandable format. Data visualization techniques, reports, presentations, or dashboards are often used to communicate the findings effectively.
- **Implementing Results:** The insights garnered from your data analysis can now be used to influence decision-making, from strategic business changes to digital marketing campaigns to scientific conclusions.

Each of these steps contributes to the comprehensive, insightful understanding of the data, enabling informed decision-making and 'storytelling' using empirical evidence.

Techniques in Data Analysis

In data analysis, there are several techniques that are commonly used to process and understand data better. Some of them include:

- **Descriptive Statistics:** These are used to describe the main features of a dataset in a quantitative manner. Descriptive statistics provide simple summaries of the sample. These definitions include measures such as mean, median, and mode for central tendency, while measures such as variance, standard deviation, and range help measure dispersion or spread in your data.
- **Inferential Statistics:** These are techniques that allow us to use data from a sample to infer or make generalizations about the population. Examples: Hypothesis testing, regression analysis, analysis of variance (ANOVA), *etc.*
- **Data Visualization:** This is the representation of data in graphical or pictorial format. It allows decision-makers to visually digest difficult concepts or identify new patterns, as well as make data more accessible. Some commonly used visuals include line graphs, bar charts, pie charts, scatter plots, heat maps, and more.
- **Correlation Analysis:** Correlation analysis is a method used to evaluate the strength and direction of the relationship between two quantitative variables. A correlation can be positive (both variables increase together), negative (one variable decreases as the other increases), or neutral (no relationship). It is often represented using a correlation coefficient that ranges between -1 and +1.

- **Regression Analysis:** This statistical process is used to estimate the relationships among variables. It includes many techniques for modeling and analyzing several variables, with the goal of understanding the relationship between a dependent variable and one or more independent variables.
- **Hypothesis Testing:** Hypothesis testing is an inferential statistical method used to test the outcome of a hypothesis performed on sample data from a larger population. The method determines whether the sample data provides sufficient evidence to reject the hypothesis.
- **Factor Analysis:** Factor Analysis is a technique used to reduce a large number of variables into fewer factors. The variables are grouped by their correlations, *i.e.*, high inter-correlations exist within each group.

Each of these techniques provides different insights and is used based on the specific requirements of the analysis you're running. By understanding and properly utilizing them, one can bring out useful patterns and insights from their data.

Introduction to Data Mining

Data Mining, often considered a subset of data analysis, goes beyond the manual efforts involved in data analysis and into the realm of automated, algorithm-driven extraction of knowledge and patterns hidden within large data sets. Data mining is not aimed at answering specific questions. Instead, it is focused on discovering new, often surprising insights in large datasets. It is a multidisciplinary field that leverages techniques from database technology, statistics, machine learning, and artificial intelligence.

Goals of Data Mining

The major goals of data mining include:

Prediction: Data mining uses one set of variables to predict unknown or future values of other variables of interest. For example, it can be used to forecast stock market trends.

Identification: Data patterns can be used to identify the existence of an item, an event, or an activity. For example, credit card companies can mine data to detect potentially fraudulent usage.

Classification: Data mining can be used to retrieve critical and relevant information about data, and metadata. This may be used to categorize different data classes or concepts.

Optimization: It can also be used to get optimization for using limited resources such as time, space, money, or materials to get the maximum efficiency.

Tasks in Data Mining

There are two types of tasks in the field of data mining:

Descriptive Task: The main idea present in the descriptive task is the use of data mining techniques to provide a better understanding and explanation of the available features that correspond to a particular dataset.

Predictive task: In the case of the predictive task, various data mining techniques are used for predicting the implicit values, which are based solely on available data set features.

How It Differs From Simple Data Analysis

While data analysis and data mining both work with data, the main difference lies in what they are used for. Data analysis is often used to test models and hypotheses on the dataset, *e.g.*, "If I provide a discount to customers during the holiday season, will profits increase?".

On the other hand, data mining uses machine learning and statistical models to uncover clandestine patterns in massive volumes of data. This can help uncover hidden patterns and relationships among different variables in the dataset, providing insights that would not be immediately obvious with simple analysis.

In other words, data analysis is used to clearly define a problem and then use the data to solve this problem. Data mining, instead, is about finding patterns and relationships in the data that may provide insights that we did not even think to consider before.

Techniques and Methods in Data Mining

Data mining involves employing various techniques to discover patterns and glean insights from large data sets. Some of the key data mining techniques are:

- **Clustering:** This is a technique used to group a set of data objects in such a way that objects in the same group (or cluster) are more similar to each other than those in other clusters. These groups or clusters can then be used to understand the data distribution, identify anomalies, or segment data for further analysis. K-Means and DBSCAN are common clustering algorithms.
- **Classification:** Classification is a technique used for predicting the class or category of given data points. It involves training a model using a dataset with

pre-defined class labels (also known as supervised learning), and then using this model to classify or predict the categories of new, unseen data. Common classification algorithms include Decision Trees, Random Forests, Naive Bayes, and Support Vector Machines (SVM).

- **Regression:** Regression analysis is a statistical process for estimating the relationships between variables, one dependent variable and one or more independent variables. It allows you to understand how the typical value of the dependent variable changes when any one of the independent variables is varied. Linear Regression and Logistic Regression are two commonly used regression techniques.
- **Association Rule Mining:** This is a technique used to identify associations or patterns among a set of items in a dataset. It's frequently used in market basket analysis, where the aim is to find associations and/or correlations amongst sets of items purchased together. The most famous algorithm for mining association rules is the Apriori algorithm.

Each of these techniques has its unique strengths and suitability for different types of tasks. Choosing the correct technique depends on your specific data mining goals: whether you're looking to categorize data, predict outcomes, identify associations, or understand data structure. Using the right data mining techniques can significantly improve the quality of insights and predictions derived from a dataset.

Data Mining Tools

There are several tools available for data mining, each offering a unique set of capabilities. Here's a brief overview of some popular ones:

- **RapidMiner:** RapidMiner is a leading data science platform providing an integrated environment for data preparation, machine learning, deep learning, text mining, and predictive analytics. It offers a user-friendly graphical user interface (GUI), meaning you can implement data mining techniques without needing to write lines of code. RapidMiner is usable in various sectors including business, industrial, and social sciences.
- **Oracle Data Mining (ODM):** Part of the Oracle Advanced Analytics Database, ODM is a comprehensive module providing powerful data mining algorithms that enable data analysts to discover insights, make predictions, and leverage their Oracle data. Oracle Data Mining allows analysts to build and deploy predictive models inside the Oracle Database to help optimize business decisions.
- **WEKA (Waikato Environment for Knowledge Analysis):** WEKA is a popular suite of machine learning software written in Java, developed at the

University of Waikato, New Zealand. It is open-source and provides comprehensive facilities for data analysis and predictive modeling. WEKA supports several standard data mining tasks, including data preprocessing, clustering, classification, regression, visualization, and feature selection.

- **KNIME:** A powerful, open-source data analytics tool, KNIME allows you to perform sophisticated statistics and data mining *via* its modular data pipelining concept. It integrates various components for machine learning and data mining through its modular data pipelining concept and provides GUI and REST APIs.
- **SAS Data Mining:** SAS is a leader in the data mining software industry. It offers a comprehensive range of statistical analysis and data mining solutions and has a highly graphical user interface that caters to all kinds of users, including data scientists, statisticians, and business analysts.

Each tool has its strengths and is better suited for specific types of tasks. The choice of the tool often depends on the size and nature of the data, the specific requirements of the task, and the skills of the user.

Real-world Applications of Data Analysis and Mining

Data analysis and data mining are being effectively used across numerous sectors, providing actionable insights and influencing decisions. Here are some real-world examples and case studies:

Healthcare

In the healthcare industry, data analysis and data mining are being utilized for predicting disease outbreaks and identifying risk factors for various health conditions. For instance, Google Flu Trends used search query data to predict influenza epidemics in real-time, faster than traditional systems managed by the Center for Disease Control and Prevention (CDC).

Finance and Banking

Banks and financial institutions use these techniques for risk modeling, fraud detection, customer segmentation, and credit scoring. American Express, for example, mines and analyzes historical transaction data to develop algorithms that predict potential churn, helping them retain customers more effectively.

Retail

Major retailers, such as Amazon and Walmart, use data mining to understand customer behavior, optimize product placements, manage inventory, and even personalize promotions and offers. Macy's uses data mining to change prices in near real-time for up to 73 million items, based on demand and inventory.

Telecommunications

Verizon, a major telecom provider, uses data mining techniques for network management and to predict churn and identify reasons. By analyzing call detail data, they can identify usage patterns, deliver tailored services, and even detect fraudulent activities.

Entertainment

Netflix, the global streaming service, uses data mining to provide personalized recommendations to millions of users, which improves user engagement and satisfaction. It famously ran the Netflix Prize competition, providing anonymized rating data and challenging data miners worldwide to improve its recommendation algorithm's accuracy.

These examples showcase how analyzing and mining large volumes of data can uncover insights that drive smarter decisions, optimize operations, and even create a competitive advantage across different sectors.

Future Trends in Data Analysis and Mining

Emerging trends in technology are reshaping the landscape of data analysis and data mining. As we become more comfortable with massive volumes of data and sophisticated algorithms, we're unlocking new possibilities and applications. Here are a few trends to keep an eye on:

- **AI and Machine Learning in Data Analysis:** Algorithms are becoming ever more efficient at mining, analyzing, and predicting data. Machine learning models are increasingly being used for prediction, classification, and clustering. Deep learning, a subfield of machine learning, is also gaining popularity due to its exceptional performance with image and language data.
- **Predictive Analytics:** Predictive analytics uses statistical algorithms and machine learning techniques to identify the likelihood of future outcomes. It's being used in diverse fields such as predicting disease outbreaks in healthcare, forecasting sales in retail, or understanding customer behavior in marketing.
- **Real-time Analytics:** As the ability to collect and process data in real-time improves, businesses can make data-informed decisions quicker than ever before. This trend is evident in sectors like finance for real-time fraud detection, or in manufacturing for real-time quality control.
- **Growing Importance of Data Privacy and Ethics:** As data use grows, so do concerns around data privacy and ethical data use. Principles of 'privacy by design', anonymization, and transparent data governance are starting to become

standard. Ensuring that data analysis and mining don't infringe on individual privacy rights or propagate bias is a crucial consideration.

In conclusion, mastering data analysis and data mining promise to unlock 'stellar insights'. As technology evolves, our ability to dig into data and extract meaningful insights continues to expand. Although the tools and techniques we use may evolve, the core principle remains the same: harnessing data to drive informed decisions and create value. From AI to real-time analytics to data ethics, the future of data analysis and data mining is brimming with potential. Getting to grips with these methods and mastering their use is more than just a valuable skill—it's the key to unlocking the power of data.

CONCLUSION

This chapter has highlighted Big Data's significant role in enhancing market forecasting, exploring its applications across various industries, and addressing its potential and challenges. While Big Data provides strategic insights and analytical depth, it also poses quality, privacy, and security challenges. Data inconsistencies or breaches can lead to inaccurate forecasts and jeopardize user trust. Future research should focus on developing advanced data-cleaning techniques and privacy-preserving analytics to ensure data integrity and security. Furthermore, integrating artificial intelligence with Big Data could automate data processing, allowing for more dynamic and precise forecasts. Interdisciplinary approaches could also enrich analyses, providing deeper insights into market dynamics and consumer behavior.

In summary, Big Data holds great promise for market forecasting but requires continuous innovation and careful management to fully realize its potential and ensure its ethical use.

REFERENCES

Acharya, A., Singh, S.K., Pereira, V., Singh, P. (2018). Big data, knowledge co-creation and decision making in fashion industry. *Int. J. Inf. Manage., 42*, 90-101.
[http://dx.doi.org/10.1016/j.ijinfomgt.2018.06.008]

Janssen, M., Van der Voort, H., Wahyudi, A. (2017). Factors influencing big data decision-making quality. *J. Bus. Res., 70*, 338-345.
[http://dx.doi.org/10.1016/j.jbusres.2016.08.007]

Sarker, I.H. (2021). Data science and analytics: an overview from data-driven smart computing, decision-making and applications perspective. *SN Computer Science, 2*(5), 377.
[http://dx.doi.org/10.1007/s42979-021-00765-8] [PMID: 34278328]

Wang, H., Xu, Z., Fujita, H., Liu, S. (2016). Towards felicitous decision making: An overview on challenges and trends of Big Data. *Inf. Sci., 367-368*, 747-765.
[http://dx.doi.org/10.1016/j.ins.2016.07.007]

CHAPTER 4

Foundations of Cryptomarket Analysis

Abstract: Chapter 4 provides a comprehensive exploration of the fundamental financial instruments in the markets—stocks, bonds, and digital currencies—and delves into their characteristics, roles, and intricacies of the crypto market. It highlights the unique attributes of each asset class, discusses their interactions within the financial ecosystem, and examines the underlying blockchain technology that supports digital currencies.

Keywords: Bonds, Blockchain technology, Cryptomarket analysis, Digital currencies, Financial instruments, Market trends, Risk management, Stocks.

INTRODUCTION

This chapter introduces the primary financial instruments that shape the global markets: stocks, bonds, and digital currencies. It details their functions, risks, and rewards, and posits how these instruments coexist within the broader financial ecosystem. The discussion extends into the realm of digital currencies, particularly focusing on blockchain technology and its revolutionary impact on financial transactions and asset management.

Previous research has extensively explored the individual roles and mechanics of stocks and bonds within the global financial framework, examining their implications for investment strategies and economic stability (Creel *et al.*, 2015). Additionally, substantial literature exists on the technological underpinnings and market dynamics of digital currencies, highlighting their potential to disrupt traditional financial systems (Gomber *et al.*, 2018; Zachariadis *et al.*, 2019). What distinguishes this study is its integrated approach, examining not only the individual characteristics and roles of these financial instruments but also their interrelations and collective impact on the global market environment. This research introduces novel insights into how traditional and modern financial instruments can be strategically aligned for optimal asset management and investment, and further delves into the implications of blockchain technology not just as a tool for transaction security but also as a foundational element that could redefine asset management practices globally.

Heng Chen

A Financial Odyssey: The Trinity of Stocks, Bonds, and Digital Currencies

Herein an overview of the three main financial instruments - stocks, bonds, and digital currencies is provided. Also, their importance and role in the financial markets are discussed.

Financial markets are vast and diverse, with a wide range of instruments that investors can use to create wealth, manage risk, and achieve their financial goals. Today, we will focus on three main categories: stocks, bonds, and digital currencies.

- **Stocks:** Stocks represent ownership shares in a company. When you buy a stock, you become a part-owner of that company, and your investment's performance is tied to the company's success or failure. Stocks are typically used for long-term growth investment strategies as history suggests they offer a higher return over the long term compared to other assets.
- **Bonds:** Bonds are essentially loans that investors make to entities like corporations or governments. When you purchase a bond, the issuer promises to pay you back the principal amount plus interest over a specific period. Bonds are generally considered less risky than stocks and are often used to generate steady income and provide portfolio diversification.
- **Digital Currencies:** A relatively new addition to the financial markets, digital currencies or cryptocurrencies are decentralized digital or virtual forms of money. The most well-known digital currency is Bitcoin, but there are thousands of others including Ethereum, Ripple, and Litecoin. Cryptocurrencies offer potential for high returns but also carry significant risks due to their volatility.

All three of these financial instruments play crucial roles in the financial markets:

Stock allows companies to raise capital to fund new projects or investments while providing individuals and institutions with a share in the company's potential profits through capital gains and dividends.

Bonds enable entities like corporations and governments to borrow money for various purposes including funding projects, managing cash flow, or refinancing debt. Investors benefit from regular interest payments and the return of the principal upon the bond's maturity.

Digital currencies, while still evolving, are playing an increasingly significant role in the financial ecosystem. They offer opportunities for high returns and portfolio diversification, and are starting to challenge traditional concepts of money and payment systems.

While each instrument serves a different purpose and caters to specific investment needs and risk tolerance, a balanced portfolio often includes a mix of these assets to manage risk and optimize returns.

Delve into the nature of stocks, their types, the means to evaluate them (fundamental & technical analysis), and their risk-reward characteristics.

Stocks, also known as shares or equities, represent ownership interests in a company. When you buy a stock, you become a shareholder, entitling you to a portion of the company's assets and earnings according to the number and type of shares held.

Stocks are generally categorized into two types:

- **Common Stocks:** These are the most commonly traded type and shareholders have voting rights in the company along with the potential to receive dividends.
- **Preferred Stocks:** Preferred shareholders have a higher claim on dividends and assets. They receive dividends before common shareholders and, in case of liquidation, have priority claims over assets. However, they generally do not have voting rights.

Evaluation of stocks can be done *via* two main analyses:

- **Fundamental Analysis:** This involves evaluating a company's financials, industry position, and market conditions to estimate the intrinsic value of the stock. If the intrinsic value is believed to be higher than the current market price, the stock is considered undervalued, making it a potential buy.
- **Technical Analysis:** Technical analysts study price movements and trading volume patterns utilizing charts and technical indicators. The premise is that historical price movements can forecast future trends.

Risk-Reward Characteristics: Investing in stocks involves a balance between risk and reward. While stocks have the potential for high returns in the form of capital gains and dividends, they also come with considerable risk. Share prices can be influenced by various factors including the company's financial health, market sentiment, and broader economic factors. During times of financial stress or market downturns, stock prices can drop significantly leading to potential losses for investors.

Taking time to understand different stocks and their risk-reward tradeoff, and learning how to evaluate them can go a long way in crafting a successful investment strategy. Choosing the right mix of stocks also plays a key role in portfolio diversification, which can further mitigate risk.

Discuss the basics of how the stock market works, its importance in the economy, and the trends affecting it currently.

The stock market provides a marketplace where buyers and sellers can negotiate prices and make trades.

Companies list their shares on a stock exchange, like the New York Stock Exchange or the NASDAQ, through a process known as Initial Public Offering (IPO). Stock prices fluctuate throughout the trading session based on supply (selling) and demand (buying).

The stock market plays a key role in the economy:

Raising Capital: It provides a platform for companies to raise capital from public investors. This capital can be used for expansion, research and development, or other corporate activities.

Wealth Creation: For investors, the stock market offers an opportunity for wealth creation. Investors can profit from stock market investments through capital gains (when they sell their stocks at a price higher than what they paid) and through dividends (a portion of the company's earnings distributed to shareholders).

Economic Indicators: The performance of the stock market is often used as a barometer of the overall health and investor sentiment of an economy, reflecting expectations of corporate and economic performance. A bullish (rising) market often signifies investor confidence and the expectation of strong economic performance. Conversely, a bearish (falling) market might denote investor pessimism and expectation of weakening economic conditions.

Current trends affecting the stock market include:

- **Technology Advancements:** Technology is rapidly changing the face of the stock market, from online trading platforms that provide instant access to markets worldwide, to algorithmic trading and robo-advisors.
- **Globalization:** Financial markets worldwide are increasingly interconnected. As a result, an event in one part of the world can significantly impact stock markets globally.
- **Market Volatility:** Current geopolitical situations, the COVID-19 pandemic, and changes in fiscal and monetary policy are causing elevated levels of market volatility.
- **Sustainability and ESG Investing:** There's a growing trend of investors looking at Environmental, Social, and Corporate Governance (ESG) factors as part of their investment decision-making process.

Understanding how the stock market works and keeping abreast of the trends affecting it can help investors navigate their investment journey in an informed manner.

Explore the world of bonds, how they work, their types, and the risk-return trade-off they present their investors with.

Bonds are a type of fixed-income instrument that represents a loan made by an investor to a borrower, typically corporate or governmental.

When you purchase a bond, you are essentially lending money to the issuer in exchange for periodic interest payments and the return of the bond's face value when it matures. The periodic interest rate paid on the bond is known as its coupon rate, while the face or par value is the amount paid to the holder at maturity.

The primary types of bonds include:

- **Government Bonds:** These are issued by national governments and are often deemed risk-free as they're backed by the creditworthiness of the issuing country.
- **Municipal Bonds:** These are issued by states, cities, or other local government entities to fund public projects.
- **Corporate Bonds:** These are issued by companies to raise capital for various business purposes. Corporate bonds typically offer higher yields to compensate for the additional risk compared to government bonds.
- **Convertible Bonds:** These are corporate bonds that can be converted into a predetermined amount of the company's equity at certain times during its life, usually at the discretion of the bondholder.

In terms of the risk-return trade-off:

Bonds are generally seen as less risky than stocks, making them a popular choice among conservative investors. The predictability of returns in the form of fixed, regular payments is an attractive feature of bonds.

However, bonds are not completely without risks. These include interest rate risk (when interest rates rise, bond prices fall), credit risk (the issuer may default on payments), and liquidity risk (you may not be able to sell the bond easily if required).

Moreover, while bonds' predictive returns can seem appealing, their returns are often lower than those of riskier assets like stocks over the long term.

Hence, understanding how bonds work, their types, and the associated risk-return trade-off is essential for developing a broad and balanced investment strategy.

The bond market, also known as the debt, credit, or fixed-income market, is a financial market where participants can issue new debt or buy and sell debt securities.

Here is how it operates:

Primary Market: This is where new bonds are issued. Governments, municipalities, and corporations sell new bonds to raise capital. This transaction takes place between the issuer and the first buyer.

Secondary Market: Once the bonds are issued, they can be traded between investors on the secondary market. The price can fluctuate due to various factors, including changes in interest rates, credit rating upgrades or downgrades, or changes in the issuer's financial health.

Interest rates play a significant role in the bond market:

Price-Interest Rate Relationship: There's an inverse relationship between bond prices and interest rates. When interest rates rise, bond prices fall, and vice versa. This is because as interest rates increase, newly issued bonds become more attractive (with higher yields) than existing bonds, which drives down the price of existing bonds.

Yield: The yield is the overall return an investor gets from a bond. It factors in both the bond's price and its interest payments. As interest rates increase, the yield on newly issued bonds increases, which in turn makes these new bonds more attractive to investors.

Current trends impacting the bond market include:

Impact of Central Bank Policies: Monetary policy set by central banks, such as the Federal Reserve in the U.S, plays a pivotal role in dictating interest rates, thereby heavily influencing the bond market.

Increase in Corporate Debt: Corporations have been taking on an increasing amount of debt, fueled by low interest rates. A highly indebted corporate sector could be a risk if there's an economic downturn.

Environmental, Social, and Governance (ESG) Bonds: There is a growing trend towards investing in ESG bonds, or bonds issued to finance projects that have positive environmental, social, and governance impacts.

Inflation-Linked Bonds: With the growing expectation of inflation due to immense monetary stimulus around the world, inflation-linked bonds are becoming popular. They offer a hedge against inflation since their principal value is adjusted based on inflation rates.

Understanding the workings of the bond market, interest rate dynamics, and current trends offers useful insights to navigate through this space.

Digital Currencies

Digital currencies, including cryptocurrencies, represent a major advancement in the financial and economic sectors. Unlike traditional currencies, these are entirely digital and utilize technologies like blockchain to secure and validate transactions.

The two most well-known digital currencies or cryptocurrencies are Bitcoin (BTC) and Ethereum (ETH).

Bitcoin (BTC) came into existence in 2009 by an unknown person or a group of people using the name Satoshi Nakamoto. Bitcoin is often referred to as digital gold due to its limited supply, similar to the scarcity of gold.

Ethereum (ETH), launched in 2015 by Vitalik Buterin, goes beyond the financial use case, providing a blockchain platform that supports smart contracts – self-executing contracts with the terms directly written into code.

Unique Features of Cryptocurrencies

Decentralization: Cryptocurrencies are not controlled by any central authority, such as a government or financial institution. This decentralization is enabled by blockchain technology, a distributed ledger enforced by a network of computers called nodes.

Limited Supply: Most cryptocurrencies, including Bitcoin, have a limited supply, creating scarcity which can drive up value.

Anonymity: While all transactions are recorded on the blockchain, the identities of the parties involved remain pseudo-anonymous. This means that while transaction data is transparent and public, the identities of the people making transactions are not always easily traceable.

Advantages

Security: Cryptocurrencies use cryptographic technology for secure transactions, reducing the risk of fraud.

Efficiency: As they are not tied to any specific country or central banking system, cryptocurrencies can enable cheaper and quicker transactions, especially for international transfers.

Investment Potential: Given their volatility, cryptocurrencies can offer significant return potential for investors ready to bear high risk.

Risks

Volatility: Cryptocurrency prices can fluctuate wildly in short periods, leading to potential financial losses.

Lack of Regulation: The absence of standard regulatory oversight can lead to an increased risk of fraud and market manipulation.

Cybersecurity Issues: Despite inherent security features, cryptocurrencies are not immune to hacking or theft.

Legal and Adoption Risks: The legal treatment of cryptocurrencies can change rapidly and vary in different jurisdictions, potentially affecting their value and acceptance.

As the world becomes increasingly digital, cryptocurrencies represent a new frontier in finance, characterized by volatility and the potential for high reward – and risk. Whether considered as part of an investment portfolio or as a utilitarian tool for transactions, it's evident that digital currencies are gaining benefits.

Explore how the digital currency market operates, the blockchain technology underpinning it, and its potential implications and trends.

The digital currency or cryptocurrency market is a platform that facilitates the trading of digital currencies. Similar to traditional financial markets, it operates round the clock, allowing the buying, selling, and exchange of digital currencies such as Bitcoin, Ethereum, and many others.

Underpinning the operation of digital currencies is **blockchain technology**. A blockchain is a type of distributed ledger technology that records all transactions made with a particular digital currency. This network is maintained by multiple 'nodes' each storing a copy of the ledger, which ensures that transactions are transparent and cannot be altered or tampered with after being verified and added to the blockchain. This enhances the security, transparency, and reliability of the digital currency.

These are some key implications and trends in the digital currency market:

- **DeFi (Decentralized Finance):** DeFi represents a shift from traditional, centralized financial systems towards a universally accessible financial system built on open, decentralized networks. It employs smart contracts on blockchains, the most common being Ethereum, and includes decentralized exchanges (DEX), lending and borrowing platforms, prediction markets, and more.
- **NFTs (Non-Fungible Tokens):** NFTs are unique digital assets that represent real-world objects like art, music, goods, and more, on the blockchain. They are gaining popularity due to their ability to certify a digital asset as unique, adding scarcity and value.
- **Cryptocurrency Regulations:** As digital currencies continue to grow and mature, regulatory bodies across the globe are focussing on them. Regulatory frameworks and legal approaches to digital currencies can have a sizable impact on their adoption and value.
- **Blockchain and Sustainability:** Blockchain technology can play a significant role in tracking and verifying sustainable practices. However, the environmental impact posed by energy-intensive processes in certain cryptocurrencies, notably Bitcoin, is also being critically examined.
- **Adoption by Institutions:** Increasingly, financial institutions, companies, and even countries (like El Salvador making Bitcoin a legal tender) are adopting digital currency, signaling its growing integration into the conventional financial system.

The operation of the digital currency market and the ever-evolving developments in blockchain technology have broad and exciting implications. While opportunities abound, the inherent volatility and uncertainties require market participants to tread with caution and make well-informed decisions.

Compare and contrast stocks, bonds, and digital currencies. Discuss their co-existence, rivalry, and interrelation, rounding up what this 'financial trinity' means to the modern investor.

Stocks, bonds, and digital currencies represent different classes of financial assets, each with its unique features, benefits, risks, and role within a diversified portfolio. Here's a comparative look at these three types of investments:

Stocks represent ownership in a company and offer the potential for high returns through capital gains and dividends. However, they are subject to market volatility and profitability of the company, making them riskier compared to bonds.

Bonds are debt securities issued by governments or corporations to raise capital. Investors who purchase bonds are essentially lending money to the issuer in return for periodic interest payments plus the return of the bond's face value at its maturity. Bonds generally offer lower returns than stocks but provide stable income and are considered less risky.

Digital Currencies, like Bitcoin and Ethereum, are a relatively new asset class. They offer the potential for high returns due to their volatility but carry significant risks, including regulatory uncertainty, and cybersecurity threats, and they can experience rapid and dramatic price swings.

These three types of investments co-exist and interact in interesting and complex ways:

Co-existence: Each one caters to different investor needs and risk appetites. Stocks are typically for those seeking growth and are willing to accept higher volatility. Bonds are for those requiring steady income with less concern for high returns. Digital currencies attract investors ready to embrace risk in return for potentially outsized gains.

Rivalry: They can act as alternatives to each other as per the market environment. For instance, in times of market volatility, investors may switch from stocks to bonds, considered a safer option. Meanwhile, digital currencies, often uncorrelated to traditional asset classes, are sometimes viewed as a 'safe-haven' or hedge.

Interrelation: Movements in these markets can influence each other. Large swings in the cryptocurrency market can affect sentiment across other financial markets, and fluctuations in traditional markets may trigger flows into or out of digital currencies.

The 'Financial Trinity' of stocks, bonds, and digital currencies is shaping the landscape of modern investing. They provide a range of options for creating a diversified and balanced portfolio tailored to an investor's specific goals, risk tolerance, and investment horizon. It is essential for investors to understand the dynamics of each and how they can impact their overall investment strategy.

Trends and Indicators: The Magic Spells of Market Analysis

The Magic Spells of Market Analysis" would encompass a fair and comprehensive understanding of trends, market analysis, and various indicators. Here's a suggested breakdown:

Trends

A trend in the simplest terms refers to the general direction in which something is developing or changing. In market analysis, a trend is identified by a series of higher highs and higher lows in an uptrend, or lower highs and lower lows in a downtrend. Recognizing these trends, their strengths, and when they might be changing is a key aspect for analysts in predicting market behavior.

Let us take for example the financial market. Both short-term traders who make numerous trades in a single day and long-term investors who buy and hold assets for years could utilize the trend concept. Traders might use technical analysis, chart patterns, trend lines, moving averages, and other techniques to assess potential trend strength and longevity. Meanwhile, long-term investors might examine the broader economic and business landscape to discern long-term trends.

Indicators

Indicators are statistical methods used to clarify or predict trends. They act as a guide, providing insights into market conditions and the direction in which the market is likely going. There are many types of indicators, including economic indicators, financial indicators, and technical indicators.

In the context of business trends, indicators could be in the form of sales growth, employee turnover rates, or profit margins, which are used to predict the financial health of a company. In the financial market, this could mean observing the gross domestic product (GDP), interest rates, or even employment rates to predict economic health.

The Crucial Role of Trends and Indicators in Market Analysis

In market analysis, trends and indicators play a decisive role in painting a clear picture of market conditions. Understanding trends can help investors make the right trading decisions at the right time, while indicators can provide quantitative measures to back up these decisions. Together, they help to form a comprehensive analysis of the market, contributing insights, predictions, and strategies beneficial to professionals across various sectors including finance, business, and economy.

Definition of Trend

A trend is a general direction in which something is developing or changing. It represents a consistent pattern over a certain period of time which can be upward (ascending), downward (descending), or sideways (horizontal).

Trends in Real Life

In our daily lives, we come across several trends. They could be in the form of fashion styles, music genres, food preferences, or social media behavior. For instance, let's consider the healthy eating trend. Over the years, there has been an increased interest in organic, plant-based foods. This has led to a surge in demand for such products, prompting supermarkets and restaurants to adapt their offerings to cater to this trend.

Trends in Cryptocurrency Market

In the cryptocurrency market, a trend refers to the overall direction of a cryptocurrency's price. It is a crucial aspect of market analysis and can significantly affect the investment decisions of traders.

For example, during the 2017 Bitcoin Bull Run, the price of Bitcoin

Various market indicators provide a snapshot of market conditions at any given time, and these indicators influence decision-making in many ways. Here's a brief explanation:

Volume: This is the number of shares or contracts traded in a security or market during a specific period. High volume often suggests strong investor interest and can indicate the start of a new trend.

Volatility: This measures the rate at which the price of an asset increases or decreases for a given set of returns. Volatility is normally used as an indicator of risk. High volatility often stands for high risk, hence it can influence decisions such as risk management and investment strategies. Fig. (**3**) displays the day-to-day percentage change in prices, representing volatility. High volatility can signal higher risk and is important for risk management strategies.

Price Momentum: This is the rate of acceleration of a stock's price. When momentum is on the rise, it often indicates a bull market. Conversely, if momentum is slowing, it may signal the onset of a bear market.

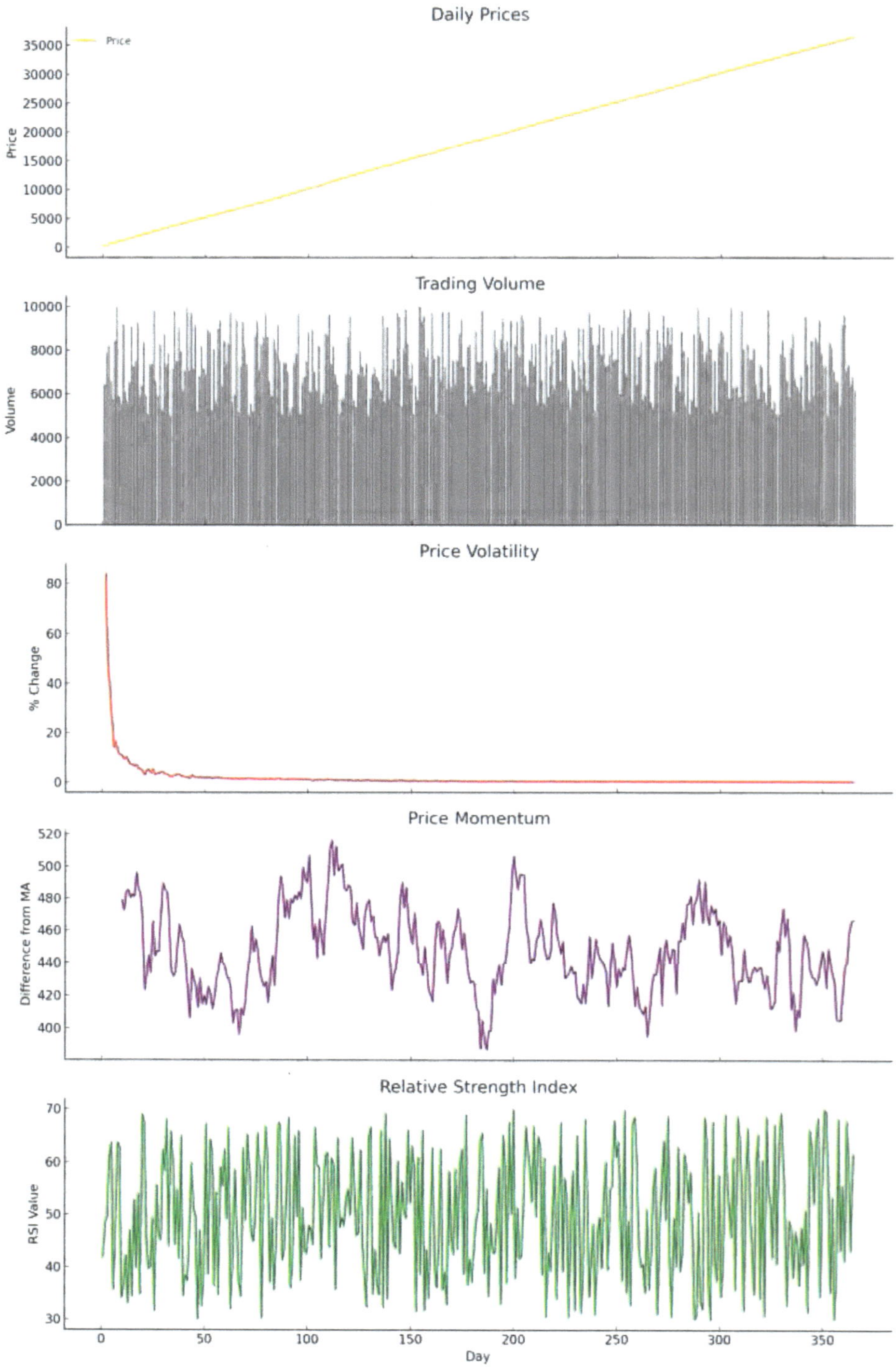

Fig. (3). Relative strength index.

Moving Averages: Moving averages smooth out price data to form a trend-following indicator. They do not predict price direction but rather define the current direction with a lag. Moving averages can aid in decision-making by giving trend direction and potential support and resistance levels. As shown in Fig. (**3**), calculated as the difference from a 10-day moving average, helps to visualize the acceleration of price changes. Rising momentum can suggest a continuing upward trend while falling momentum might indicate a potential bearish reversal.

Relative Strength Index (RSI): The RSI is a momentum oscillator that measures the speed and change of price movements. It helps identify overbought or oversold conditions in a market. The RSI values range between 30 and 70 in this simulation, indicating neither overbought nor oversold conditions consistently. It is used to identify potential reversal points based on market conditions being overbought or oversold.

Understanding these indicators can assist in making informed decisions like when to buy or sell, identifying market trends, and managing investment risks.

Remember, these are just a few examples. There are many more useful market indicators out there, each providing unique insights. The key is to use them wisely based on your specific needs and strategies.

The Combination of Trends and Indicators

Understanding both trends and indicators separately is crucial, but combining them for effective market analysis is truly where the magic happens. This combo allows investors and stakeholders to make more informed decisions. Let's break it down:

Identifying the Trend: The first step in the process involves identifying the current trend of the market. This could be an uptrend (increasing prices), a downtrend (decreasing prices), or a sideways trend (fluctuating within a range). This can be done visually by looking at a chart over time, or mathematically using trend lines or moving averages.

Applying Market Indicators: Once the trend is identified, we could turn to market indicators for further insight. These can be things like volume, volatility, momentum, or RSI. These indicators may help validate the identified trend, identify possible points of reversal, or even highlight potential trading opportunities.

For example, let us say we have identified an uptrend. If the volume indicator also increases, it strengthens our confidence in the trend, indicating that the movement has strong investor interest and might continue.

Smart Decision Making: With a solid idea about the trend and the confirming behaviour of indicators, we might then make a more informed decision about buying, selling, or holding.

Regular Updating and Analysis: The market is a dynamic entity that changes frequently. So, our understanding of trends and indicators needs to be updated accordingly.

Remember, no single indicator or trend can provide 100% accurate predictions. The idea is to increase the probability of success by making informed decisions based on the combination of multiple trends and indicators. Doing extensive research and seeking professional advice is always recommended for serious investments.

Example 1: Tech Stock Boom:

Consider the case of the technology sector boom from 2017-2020. Technology companies' stocks were in a clear uptrend during this period, with prices continually rising. Major tech stocks' prices like Amazon, Google, and Apple were increasing, which identifies an uptrend.

In this case, you could apply the Relative Strength Index (RSI) and Volume as your market indicators. The RSI showed that tech stocks were overbought during most of this period, but the volume was also very high, showing strong investor interest. Hence, despite the high RSI, the strength of the trend and the high volume could have suggested that it was still a good time to buy, and indeed those who did often experienced significant returns.

Example 2: The Housing Bubble Burst of 2008:

The 2008 housing market crash is an example of a severe market downturn. Property prices were in a clear downtrend during this period. This is an instance where being able to identify a trend and use indicators effectively could have helped to minimize losses.

In this case, the Moving Average convergence divergence (MACD) could serve as a beneficial market indicator. The MACD is a trend-following momentum indicator that shows the relationship between two moving averages of a security's price. It triggers technical signals when it crosses above (to buy) or below (to sell) its signal line. The MACD crossover signaled a sell recommendation early enough in 2007, and those who followed this advice would've been saved from the worst of the crash.

Of course, these situations are often more complex in reality, and there is always risk involved in market investments, but these examples illustrate how trends and indicators can be used together to inform decision-making in different scenarios.

As we enter deeper into the digital age, the way we analyze market trends and indicators is on the verge of significant changes fueled by advancements in Data Analysis, Artificial Intelligence (AI), and Machine Learning (ML):

Automated Market Analysis: Both AI and ML can automate the entire process of market analysis. Traders and investors will no longer have to manually study trends or indicators; instead, AI programs can do the work around the clock and alert humans when necessary. This not only improves speed and efficiency but also greatly reduces the chance of human error.

Predictive Analytics: Predictive analytics use historical data, statistical algorithms, and ML techniques to predict future trends and movements. This will allow us to anticipate market trends and movements before they happen, providing a significant advantage.

Customized Indicators: With AI, it is possible to design more personalized and accurate market indicators based on an individual's trading behavior and history, enhancing the decision-making process.

High-Frequency Trading: In financial market trends and indicators, time plays a critical role. Being able to react in milliseconds can be the difference between profit and loss. AI algorithms have the advantage of speed over any human trader.

Sentiment Analysis: AI can process and analyze unstructured data like news articles, social media posts, and even speeches to gauge market sentiment, thus identifying trends from mass behavior.

Despite these advancements, it is important to remember that as powerful as these tools are, they are not foolproof. They are only as good as the data they're fed, and they still require a level of human oversight. It's also important to account for market factors that cannot be measured or anticipated, such as sudden political changes or natural disasters.

So, while the future of market analysis looks set to be dominated by technology, the human touch will remain a crucial element.

In conclusion, it is apparent that trends and indicators play an integral role in market analysis. They provide valuable insights into the behavior of markets, enable participants to make informed decisions and offer a lens through which we can potentially forecast future market movement.

Throughout this document, we have attempted to shed light on why trends and indicators can indeed be considered the magic spells of market analysis. They provide a systematic, data-driven way of evaluating markets, which, coupled with proper interpretation and sound judgement, can be instrumental in effective decision-making.

We examined how understanding the nuances of different market conditions, along with the ability to apply relevant indicators, can result in a holistic view of the market's heartbeat. The carefully selected examples were meant to showcase potential real-life applications of these concepts.

Looking forward, the advancement in technology, particularly in the fields of AI and Machine Learning, is revolutionizing the way we analyze trends and indicators by further automating these processes, offering predictive analytics, and even personalizing market indicators.

However, as we welcome these technological advances, it is important to note that human oversight and judgement will always be necessary. Trends and indicators are tools that offer a systematic approach to understanding market behavior. The real magic spell, perhaps, is the ability to apply these tools effectively while also considering the unquantifiable and unpredictable aspects of the market.

The Emergence of Cryptomarket Analysis

The emergence of cryptocurrency analysis within the financial landscape represents a significant paradigm shift, introducing new dynamics and challenges for investors and analysts alike. This section delves into the foundations of crypto market analysis, exploring its unique characteristics, methods, and implications.

Understanding Cryptocurrency Analysis

Cryptocurrency analysis involves evaluating digital currencies like Bitcoin, Ethereum, and others to make informed investment decisions. Unlike traditional financial instruments, cryptocurrencies operate within a decentralized ecosystem, driven by blockchain technology and governed by different principles.

Key Components of Cryptomarket Analysis

Blockchain Fundamentals: Understanding the underlying technology of blockchain is fundamental to analyzing cryptocurrencies. Blockchain serves as a distributed ledger that records all transactions transparently and immutably. Analyzing blockchain data provides insights into transaction volumes, network activity, and the overall health of a cryptocurrency.

Market Sentiment: Cryptocurrency markets are highly influenced by investor sentiment and market psychology. Analyzing social media trends, online forums, and sentiment indicators can provide valuable insights into market sentiment, helping investors anticipate market movements.

Technical Analysis: Similar to traditional markets, technical analysis plays a crucial role in crypto market analysis. Analysts use various technical indicators, chart patterns, and trading signals to identify trends, support and resistance levels, and potential entry and exit points.

Fundamental Analysis: While fundamental analysis in the crypto market differs from traditional markets, it still involves evaluating factors such as the technology behind the cryptocurrency, its use case, development activity, adoption rate, regulatory environment, and the team behind the project.

Evaluating Cryptocurrencies

Risk Assessment

Volatility: Cryptocurrencies are known for their high volatility, which presents both opportunities and risks for investors. Understanding the factors driving volatility and implementing risk management strategies are essential for navigating the crypto market.

Regulatory Risk: Regulatory uncertainty remains a significant risk factor in the crypto market. Changes in regulatory frameworks or government policies can have a profound impact on cryptocurrency prices and market sentiment.

Security Risks: Cybersecurity threats, including hacking, phishing attacks, and wallet vulnerabilities, pose significant risks to investors and cryptocurrency platforms. Assessing the security measures implemented by cryptocurrency projects is crucial for mitigating security risks.

Potential Rewards

Growth Potential: Cryptocurrencies offer the potential for exponential growth, driven by factors such as technological innovation, adoption by mainstream institutions, and increasing retail investor interest.

Portfolio Diversification: Including cryptocurrencies in a diversified investment portfolio can provide exposure to an emerging asset class with low correlation to traditional markets, potentially enhancing overall portfolio returns.

Innovative Use Cases: Beyond investment opportunities, cryptocurrencies enable innovative use cases such as decentralized finance (DeFi), non-fungible tokens (NFTs), and blockchain-based applications, which could revolutionize various industries.

Current Trends and Developments

Institutional Adoption

Institutional Investment: The influx of institutional capital into the crypto market, driven by the growing acceptance of cryptocurrencies as an asset class, has contributed to increased liquidity and market maturity.

Corporate Adoption: Several companies have begun to integrate cryptocurrencies into their business models, accepting Bitcoin as a form of payment or investing in digital assets as part of their treasury reserves.

Regulatory Evolution

Regulatory Clarity: Regulatory clarity is gradually emerging in various jurisdictions, providing greater certainty for market participants and fostering mainstream adoption of cryptocurrencies.

Compliance Standards: The development of regulatory frameworks and compliance standards aims to address concerns related to investor protection, anti-money laundering (AML), and know-your-customer (KYC) requirements in the crypto market.

Technological Innovation

Layer 2 Solutions: Layer 2 scaling solutions, such as the Lightning Network for Bitcoin and the Ethereum 2.0 upgrade, aim to improve scalability, and transaction throughput, and reduce network congestion in blockchain networks.

Interoperability: Projects focusing on interoperability between different blockchain networks seek to overcome fragmentation and enable seamless transfer of value and data across multiple platforms.

Conclusion: Navigating the Cryptomarket Landscape

As the crypto market continues to evolve, understanding its complexities and dynamics is essential for investors seeking to capitalize on emerging opportunities while managing associated risks. Cryptocurrency analysis represents a fusion of traditional financial analysis techniques with innovative approaches tailored to the unique characteristics of digital assets. By embracing a multidimensional approach to crypto market analysis and staying abreast of evolving trends and developments, investors can navigate the crypto market landscape with confidence and resilience.

CONCLUSION

The chapter concludes by asserting the significance of understanding these diverse financial instruments for achieving a balanced investment portfolio. It underscores the dynamic nature of the financial markets, influenced heavily by technological advancements and regulatory changes, particularly in the realm of digital currencies. The insights provided aim to equip investors with the knowledge to navigate the complexities of the modern financial landscape effectively.

In conclusion, the insights provided aim to equip investors with the knowledge to navigate the complexities of the modern financial landscape effectively. However, this analysis may have limitations due to the rapidly evolving nature of digital currencies and the unpredictable shifts in global markets, which introduce a level of uncertainty that could not be fully addressed. Furthermore, the interplay between these financial instruments and emerging technologies, such as AI and blockchain, warrants deeper examination. Future research could explore the implications of regulatory changes and further technological advancements, and their impacts on market stability and investor behavior. This continued inquiry will be crucial for developing more robust financial models and investment strategies that can adapt to the rapidly changing economic landscape.

REFERENCES

Creel, J., Hubert, P., Labondance, F. (2015). Financial stability and economic performance. *Econ. Model., 48*, 25-40.
[http://dx.doi.org/10.1016/j.econmod.2014.10.025]

Gomber, P., Kauffman, R.J., Parker, C., Weber, B.W. (2018). On the fintech revolution: Interpreting the forces of innovation, disruption, and transformation in financial services. *J. Manage. Inf. Syst., 35*(1), 220-265.

[http://dx.doi.org/10.1080/07421222.2018.1440766]

Zachariadis, M., Hileman, G., Scott, S.V. (2019). Governance and control in distributed ledgers: Understanding the challenges facing blockchain technology in financial services. *Inf. Organ., 29*(2), 105-117.
[http://dx.doi.org/10.1016/j.infoandorg.2019.03.001]

CHAPTER 5

Practical Application of the Catboost Model

Abstract: Chapter 5 discusses the practical application of the Catboost model in handling big data for cryptocurrency market forecasting. It details the process of model building, from defining the problem and data collection to preprocessing, feature selection, model selection, training, evaluation, and deployment. The chapter emphasizes the importance of each step in transforming raw data into actionable insights and provides a comprehensive guide on implementing Catboost models effectively.

Keywords: Catboost, Cryptocurrency forecasting, Data preprocessing, Feature selection, Model building, Model selection, Model training, Model evaluation, Model deployment, Machine learning.

INTRODUCTION

This chapter delves into the practical aspects of applying the Catboost model to predict cryptocurrency market trends. It outlines the sequence of steps necessary for transforming raw data into a predictive model, emphasizing the importance of a structured approach to model building. The chapter aims to equip readers with the knowledge to effectively manage and utilize big data, enhancing their forecasting capabilities in the volatile cryptocurrency market.

Previous research has extensively explored various machine learning models for financial forecasting, often focusing on traditional algorithms like ARIMA, SVM, and neural networks (Sheta *et al.*, 2015; Siami-Namini and Namin, 2018). These studies have provided valuable insights into pattern recognition and anomaly detection within complex market data (Chhajer *et al.*, 2022). However, less attention has been paid to advanced ensemble methods, particularly in handling categorical variables in financial datasets, which can significantly influence model performance due to their inherent noise and sparsity.

The innovative aspect of this research lies in its application of the Catboost model, which is uniquely suited to manage categorical data effectively with its sophisticated handling of feature transformations and its ability to prevent overfitting. This research not only bridges the gap in applying gradient boosting

Heng Chen

techniques to cryptocurrency predictions but also introduces a systematic approach to feature engineering and model validation that could set a new standard for predictive accuracy in this domain.

As shown in Table **6**, the steps in model building include the following: Defining the Problem, which involves clarifying the problem, setting objectives, understanding data requirements, and defining success metrics; Data Collection, which focuses on identifying data sources, selecting collection methods, ensuring data quality, and considering legal and ethical implications; Data Preprocessing, where missing data is handled, outliers are detected and managed, data is transformed, features are encoded, and the data is partitioned; Feature Selection, which involves choosing relevant features using filter, wrapper, embedded methods, and dimensionality reduction techniques; Model Selection, which is the process of selecting the appropriate machine learning model based on the problem, data nature, and constraints; Model Training, which includes training the selected model with the training dataset, tuning hyperparameters, and implementing validation strategies; Model Evaluation, which tests the model on separate data and uses relevant metrics to assess performance, considering baseline comparisons; and Model Deployment, which involves deploying the model in a production environment, monitoring performance, maintaining data infrastructure, and updating the model as needed.

Table 6. Steps in model building.

Step	Description
Defining the Problem	Clarifying the problem, setting objectives, understanding data requirements, and defining success metrics.
Data Collection	Identifying data sources, selecting collection methods, ensuring data quality, and considering legal/ethical implications.
Data Preprocessing	Handling missing data, detecting and managing outliers, transforming data, encoding features, and partitioning data.
Feature Selection	Choosing relevant features using filter, wrapper, embedded methods, and dimensionality reduction techniques.
Model Selection	Selecting the appropriate machine learning model based on the problem, data nature, and constraints.
Model Training	Training the selected model with the training dataset, tuning hyperparameters, and implementing validation strategies.
Model Evaluation	Testing the model on separate data, using relevant metrics to assess performance, and considering baseline comparisons.
Model Deployment	Deploying the model in a production environment, monitoring performance, maintaining data infrastructure, and updating the model as needed.

THE METAMORPHOSIS OF DATA: STEPS IN MODEL BUILDING

In today's world, data is generated at an unprecedented scale and pace. This explosion of data presents both challenges and opportunities for organizations seeking competitive advantages from their raw data. Navigating these colossal amounts of data and extracting insightful knowledge necessitates a dramatic transformation, hence the term "Data Metamorphosis."

Data Metamorphosis, in essence, is an umbrella term encapsulating the whole process of converting raw, complex data into meaningful, actionable knowledge. And one of the key components of this transformative journey is Model Building.

Model Building involves developing statistical or mathematical structures that quantify patterns identified in the data. It's akin to creating a virtual simulacrum of the real world based on the data at hand. This simulacrum, or model, then serves as the gateway through which we glean insights, predictions, and strategies from our raw data.

The importance of model building in data analysis can hardly be overstated. Without appropriate models, data remains an unwieldy sea of numbers, far from the insightful knowledge we seek.

In the following sections, we'll journey through the consecutive stages of model building which will include: Defining the problem, collecting the data, preprocessing the data, feature selection, model selection, training the model, evaluating the model, and finally, deploying the model. By breaking down the process into these distinct stages, we can better understand the transformation of our raw data into a fully-fledged, functioning model.

The importance of clearly defining the problem you're trying to solve Identify your goals, the kind of data you'll need, and the results you're hoping to achieve.

Before diving headfirst into the data, it is crucial to clearly define the problem you are trying to solve. This will be the guiding principle for your entire model-building journey. It influences the kind of data you seek, the type of model you might build, and how you validate its success.

Firstly, identifying your goals can help align your efforts and streamline your focus.Articulate about what you want to predict or understand from the data. Are you looking to predict future sales, classify emails as spam or not, or understand factors that influence customer churn? The way you frame your problem will dictate the rest of the processes in model building.

Getting clarity on the type of data you will need is also a key step in problem definition. For example, if you're working on a sales forecast model, the kind of data you'll need might include previous sales data, market trends, seasonal factors, or even weather conditions. You should not only think about the scope/type of data, but also its format (numerical, categorical, timestamps, *etc.*) and possible sources (in-house databases, external data APIs, public datasets, *etc.*).

Lastly, have a clear idea about what success looks like for your model. Is it having the model accurately predict a certain percentage of future sales? Or reducing spam emails in your users' inboxes by a given factor? Setting these benchmarks early in the process can help you measure your model's performance effectively later on. Be warned though, that unrealistic or ill-defined success markers can lead to misleading conclusions about your model's performance.

In summary, when defining your problem, think about its goal and the context in which the model will be used, the relevant data you will need, and the criteria that would be used to judge its performance. Remember, the clearer the problem statement, the smoother your model-building experience.

The Process of Gathering Data for Modeling

Data Collection

Data collection is the next important step in the process of model building. This entails not only accumulating raw data but also making sure it's the right kind of data and of sufficient quality for your modeling task. Here are the key aspects:

Determining Data Sources: Depending on the problem definition, there'll be a variety of potential data sources. These can include internal databases, transaction logs, remote sensors, public data repositories, social media feeds, and even data vendors who specifically deal with acquiring and selling pertinent data. You must identify the reliable and relevant sources for your required data.

Data Collection Methods: With the sources identified, the next task is choosing the appropriate method(s) to gather the data. This can range from downloading a publicly available dataset, querying an internal database, scraping web pages, conducting surveys, or even purchasing data from vendors. The method will strongly depend on the data source and the type/format of data required.

Quality Check: Poor data quality can lead to poor model performance and misleading insights. Therefore, it is essential that your collected data undergoes an initial data quality check to catch any serious issues early on and look for inconsistencies, missing values, outliers, duplicate entries, and irrelevant data.

The specific checks might vary based on the nature of your data and the problem at hand.

Legal and Ethical Considerations: This is crucial especially when handling sensitive or personal data. Always ensure that your data collection process complies with any data privacy laws and ethical guidelines pertinent to your region or industry.

Storage and Management: Finally, think about how you'll store the collected data. Depending on your organization's data strategy and the volume of data, this could be anything from a simple spreadsheet, a local database, or even a large-scale cloud-based data warehouse.

To summarize, data collection for modeling is not a simple task of amassing numbers. It requires thoughtful consideration of the sources, collection methods, data quality, ethical implications, and storage management. Investing time in this step can pay off with smoother modeling processes and more robust results down the line.

Data Preprocessing

Data preprocessing is an indispensable step in model building; it is the stage where the raw data is transformed and refined into a format suitable for modeling. Even if the most advanced model is selected, the results will not be reliable if the data fed into it is unorganized, noisy, or inconsistent. Here's what this stage entails:

Handling Missing Data: Almost every real-world dataset contains missing values due to various reasons. It is critical to handle these missing values wisely as they can lead to misleading results. Techniques for handling missing data include simple methods like deletion (if the proportion is small) imputation (replacing the missing value with a statistical measure), or more complex methods like regression imputation or machine learning methods. The choice depends on the nature and extent of the missing data.

Outlier Detection: Outliers are values that are significantly different from other observations. They might be due to variability in the data or possible errors. Outliers can significantly impact your model's accuracy, so it is crucial to identify and handle them. Detection methods can be statistical (like Z-score or IQR) or visual (such as box plots or scatter plots), and treatments can vary from removing them to applying transformation techniques.

Data Transformation: Your data may require transformation for a number of reasons like dealing with skewed distributions, converting categorical data into numerical format, standardizing or normalizing data, feature scaling for algorithms sensitive to the scale of variables, *etc.* This step prepares your data to be more 'digestible' for your model.

Feature Encoding: Machine learning models require input data to be in numerical format, but not all your collected data will be numerical. Variables like categories, classes, labels, *etc.* need to be converted into a numerical format that models can understand. This is usually done through various encoding techniques like one-hot encoding, label encoding, *etc.*

Data Partitioning: Finally, you will also split your data into at least two subsets: a training set and a test set. Some methodologies also use a third, validation set. This allows you to train and tune your model on one set of data, and then test its performance on unseen data, which gives a more realistic gauge of its predictive performance.

Remember, garbage in is garbage out - the decision you make during preprocessing will directly affect the effectiveness of your analyses, so invest wisely in making your data as clean, well-structured, and robust as possible.

Feature Selection

In the context of model building, a “feature” is an individual measurable property or characteristic of the phenomena being observed. It is essentially a column in your dataset. For example, if you are building a model to predict housing prices, features might include the house's square footage, number of bedrooms, location, age, *etc.*

Feature selection is the process of choosing the most relevant features in your data. “Most relevant” can depend on many things: the question you are trying to answer, the model you are using, or other domain-specific criteria. Effective feature selection has several benefits: it can improve your model's performance, reduce overfitting, enhance the model's interpretability, and reduce training time.

Here are some common methods for feature selection:

Filter Methods: These are simple, quick methods that look at each feature's individual characteristics and select features based on statistical measures. Variance, chi-square, and correlation coefficient calculations can be used. These methods are generally used as a preprocessing step.

Wrapper Methods: They use trial and error to find the best set of features. They train models with various feature subsets and select the one that performs the best. Common methods include forward selection, backward selection, and recursive feature elimination. Wrapper methods are usually computationally expensive.

Embedded Methods: They perform feature selection as part of the model training process, such as decision trees and lasso regression. These techniques provide a balance between efficiency and effectiveness.

Dimensionality Reduction Techniques: These techniques, like Principal Component Analysis (PCA), create new combinations of features that maintain most of the information, but with fewer dimensions.

Remember, the goal of feature selection is to choose the best set of features that improves your model's performance according to your problem and model needs. Patience, intuition, and a fair degree of trial and error usually play a big role in this process.

Model Selection

Once you've prepared your data and selected the best features, the next stage in the process is Model Selection. This is the process by which you choose the type of model that you'll apply to your data.

There are a plethora of models to choose from, each with its own strengths, weaknesses, and assumptions. Here are some popular types of machine learning models:

Linear Regression: It is useful if you're trying to predict a continuous outcome variable (*e.g.*, house price) from one or more predictor variables.

Logistic Regression: This is used when the dependent variable is binary or dichotomous, like yes/no, true/false, or success/failure.

Decision Trees/Random Forest: These are versatile models that can work with non-linear relationships and can handle both continuous and categorical variables.

Support Vector Machines (SVM): SVMs are powerful for complex but small- or medium-sized datasets. They are especially good at dealing with high-dimensional data.

Neural Networks: Neural networks, particularly deep learning models, are excellent for complex tasks like image and speech recognition or natural language processing but require large amounts of data and computational power.

Clustering Models: If you're not trying to predict an outcome but rather understand patterns and structures in your data, unsupervised models like K-means clustering might be the right choice.

The model you choose will be influenced by your specific problem, the nature of your data, and the constraints of your situation (*i.e.*, time, computational resources, data). Typically, you would experiment with multiple models and choose the one that best meets your needs based on their performance.

It is also important to remember that no model will be perfect, rather it is about finding the model that offers the best trade-off between bias and variance, is interpretable, and meets your specific needs. It is both an art and a science – constituting statistically driven decisions and empirical experimentation.

Model Training

Once you've selected the model that best fits your data, the next step is to train that model using the training dataset. This is where your model learns the relationship between the features and the target variable. The specifics of how training works and which parameters are important can depend heavily on the type of model you're using.

Model training goes hand in hand with model validation, which helps control the quality of your model. Here are some items to consider:

Training data: You use this portion of your dataset to fit the model. It is important to feed the model with quality, representative data, as it will learn and make predictions based on this information.

Learning Algorithm: Depending on the model, a specific learning algorithm is used. For instance, in linear regression, the learning algorithm seeks to find coefficients that minimize the sum of squared errors in the predicted *vs*. actual target variable.

Hyperparameter Tuning: Certain parameters in the model are not learned from the data and are set before the training process. These are known as hyperparameters. Examples might include the learning rate in a neural network or the depth of a decision tree. They are often selected through trial and error and can significantly impact your model's performance.

Validation Strategies: There's always a risk that your model will simply memorize the training data (overfitting) and perform poorly on new, unseen data. Validation strategies help ensure your model is truly learning useful patterns. The typical method is to split your dataset into a training set and a validation set and monitor the model's performance on the validation set during training. Cross-validation, where the train-test split is performed several times in different ways and the model's performance is averaged, is another common advanced technique.

Early Stopping: In many model-building strategies, it can be wise to stop training before the model fits the training data too well, which can result in overfitting. Monitoring errors on the validation set can help identify this point.

At the end of the day, the aim is to produce a model that can accurately make predictions when presented with new, similar data. Legends aside, there is no 'magic wand' approach that works for all datasets or problems. Good model training often involves a healthy amount of experimentation, evaluation, and iteration.

Model Evaluation

After training your model, it is time to evaluate how well it performs. Here is what you need to know:

Testing Data: Ideally, testing should be done on a separate dataset that the model has not seen during training. This helps ensure that your evaluation metrics truly reflect how the model will perform on unseen data.

Evaluation Metrics: The metric you use to evaluate your model will depend on the type and objective of the model. For regression models (predicting a continuous number), common metrics include Mean Absolute Error (MAE), Mean Squared Error (MSE), and R-squared. For classification models (predicting a category), you might use accuracy, precision, recall, F1 score, or Area Under the ROC Curve (AUC-ROC). For clustering models, inertia or silhouette coefficient can be useful.

Understanding the Metrics: Understanding what your evaluation metrics represent is crucial in interpreting model performance. For instance, a high R-squared value in a regression model means it explains a large proportion of the variability in the outcome. In a classification model, high precision means that when your model predicts a positive result, it is likely to be correct. But just using precision may be misleading if your model frequently fails to predict positive results that are in fact positive (low recall). Often, a combination of metrics provides a more comprehensive view of model performance.

Baseline Comparison: It is also helpful to compare your model's performance to a simple baseline model. This could be a model that always predicts the mean outcome or a “null model” that only uses intercept terms.

Consider Overfitting and Underfitting: Overfit models might have great metrics on the training data but poor performance on the test data. Underfit models might perform poorly on both because they have not learned enough from the training data.

Model evaluation is not only about attaining high scores on metrics, but also about understanding those metrics, considering overfitting/underfitting, and comparing with simple baselines. This process helps validate and fine-tune your model before you use it to predict outcomes in the real world.

Model Deployment

After training and testing your model, the final step is to bring it into a production environment - this is known as model deployment. Deploying your model allows it to make predictions from new, unseen data.

Here are some points to consider:

Deployment Methods: Depending on your use case, deploying a model might mean integrating it into a production software system, compiling it in a report, or making it available through an API so that other software can interact with it. Cloud platforms also offer services to automate the deployment of machine learning models, like AWS Sagemaker, Google AI Platform, or Microsoft Azure ML Studio.

Monitoring Performance: Just because a model is deployed doesn't mean its lifecycle ends. It is vital to continuously monitor its performance. Over time, changes to the underlying population or the relationships between variables might deteriorate the model's original predictive accuracy, a phenomenon known as "model drift". By monitoring your model's ongoing performance, you'll be able to identify such issues early on.

Updating the Model: If you find that your model's performance is declining, or if new data becomes available, you might need to update or "retrain" your model. This might mean going back to the original dataset and adding more recent data, or it could involve adjusting parameters or even changing the type of model being used.

Maintaining Data Infrastructure: To support regular updates, it's crucial to maintain a robust data infrastructure that allows for the easy ingestion of new data, as well as the maintenance of historical data for model auditing, retraining, and comparison.

Consider Data Drift: Data drift refers to changes in the input data characteristics, which might lead to a decrease in the accuracy of the model's predictions. Constant vigilance for data drift can help ensure continued model performance.

Model deployment bridges the gap between prototype models and models that provide real-world insights. It is not merely the final stage of a model's lifecycle but instead a new phase where it starts interacting with real-world data necessitating continuous monitoring, maintenance, and improvements. Achieving a balance between model performance, model robustness, and time to market can mark the success of a model's deployment.

Conclusion

We've taken quite the journey, haven't we? From raw, unorganized data to a polished, insightful model - it's the perfect example of what we referred to earlier as "Data Metamorphosis". Just as a caterpillar undergoes a transformation to become a butterfly, our data has been refined and reshaped through multiple stages to finally emerge as a valuable, decision-making tool.

We commenced with defining the problem - figuring out what we want from our data. Then we delved into the process of gathering the relevant data, followed by the critical step of preprocessing the data, ensuring its quality and readiness for the subsequent stages.

Next, we looked at feature selection, which honed in on the most significant components of our data. Then we dealt with the challenging task of selecting the model best suited for our processed data. After a careful pick, it was time to train our model, validating it and tuning it along the way.

We then moved to test our model, using relevant metrics to analyze its performance. Finally, we focused on the deployment of the model for practical use, not forgetting the ongoing necessity to assess, update, and manage the model to ensure its continued significance and efficacy.

It is a rigorous and systematic process, but it is one that harnesses the power of data, transforming it into something more potent and insightful. This metamorphosis symbolizes what model building is all about: a meticulously crafted, step-by-step journey through which rough, complex data evolves into meaningful, action-oriented knowledge.

Remember that each stage in this transformative journey has its unique intricacies and challenges, but with careful execution, the result is robust, insightful models, ready to take on the world's data challenges. With this walkthrough in hand, you're well on your way to charting your data's metamorphosis too. Here's to successful model building!

FEATURE ENGINEERING: THE ARTISTRY OF DATA

Introduction: Begin with an overview of the concept of feature engineering, the critical role it plays in the process of data analysis, and its relationship with model performance.

Introduction

Data is the fundamental raw material of the machine learning industry, but its raw form does not often carry much value. Much like the process of a sculptor turning a rough stone into beautiful artwork, the process of finessing raw data into a form that a machine learning model can appreciate is true art — this art is known as “Feature Engineering”.

Feature engineering is the practice of transforming raw data into features, or input variables, that better represent the underlying patterns in the data to the predictive models. It is about expressing raw data in terms of the factors that influence the behavior you are trying to observe.

In essence, these features provide a more informative, clearer, or more compact view of the problem to the learning algorithms, leading to improved model accuracy.

The potential of feature engineering is best captured by the Machine Learning adage: “Coming up with features is difficult, time-consuming, and requires expert knowledge. 'Applied machine learning' is basically feature engineering.”

From enhancing model performance and interpretability to reducing computational needs and aiding in handling complex unstructured data, feature engineering indeed claims a hefty stake in the successful application of machine learning algorithms.

In the following sections, we will delve deeper into the heart of feature engineering; understanding its different types, applying various techniques, examining real-world examples, discussing challenges, and looking into the prospect of automated feature engineering. This journey will enhance our understanding of how the artistry of feature engineering brings value to raw data and thereby, fosters better predictive models in the world of machine learning.

Understanding Features: Discussing the features of data modeling and highlighting the difference between raw data and features.

Understanding Features

In the realm of machine learning and data modeling, 'features' represent the measurable attributes or properties of the observations we're interested in. If you consider each observation as an entity (like a person, a transaction, or an event), features are the components that describe the characteristics of these entities.

For example, if you're building a machine learning model to predict housing prices, your features would include attributes such as the square footage of the house, the number of bedrooms, the age of the house, its location, and so on. Here, each feature contributes information about each house in your data that the model will learn from.

Raw data, on the other hand, is the unprocessed, unfiltered information that you initially gather. In the housing prices example, raw data could be a logged record of every real estate transaction in a city, containing all kinds of information, without structure or organization, and potentially filled with errors or inconsistencies.

Feature engineering is the process of distilling raw, noisy, and voluminous data into a set of meaningful, structured, and often simpler features that can be ingested by a machine learning model. Essentially, it is the act of crafting the raw data into a language that the machine learning algorithms can understand and draw insights from.

While raw data might be full of noise and irrelevant information, a well-engineered feature encapsulates key pieces of information in a format that is most conducive to learning. It is through these features that our models can discern patterns, make predictions, and provide actionable insights.

Moving forward in our discussion, we will discover how the art and science of feature engineering can transform raw data into these valuable features.

Importance of Feature Engineering

Feature engineering is often considered one of the “secret weapons” in the world of machine learning and predictive modeling. It might not be as glamorous as designing and tuning cutting-edge machine learning models, but its importance cannot be overstated. Here are some key reasons:

Improving Model Performance: Often, raw data does not exist in a form that optimally represents the underlying problem of the predictive models. However, using engineered features, models can often more easily recognize underlying patterns. A carefully selected set of features can improve the predictive strength of almost any model, be it simple linear models or sophisticated neural networks.

Enhancing Interpretability: Well-crafted features can also make the model more understandable. If the features map onto intuitive and meaningful aspects of the domain, then when they are used in a model, it is easier to explain what the model is doing. For instance, it is easier to comprehend a model that uses "total rooms" as a feature rather than raw real estate data.

Reducing Computational Needs: By distilling unrelenting volumes of raw data into a concise set of informative features, we can reduce the amount of data that the model needs to process. This can lead to significant savings in terms of computational resources and time, especially in large-scale or real-time applications.

Enhancing Generalizability: Feature engineering can also help to reduce overfitting, which is when a model is too complex and learns the noise in the data rather than the signal. Meaningful, noise-free features can help models avoid overfitting and improve their ability to generalize from the training data to new, unseen data.

In the end, good features expose the underlying structure of the problem to the model, thereby enabling it to find a solution. They bridge the gap between the raw data and the insights we seek. As such, effective feature engineering often plays a significant role in the success of data science projects. In spite of the advancements in automated feature engineering, the human touch in designing features continues to hold its place, making it as much an art as it is a science.

Types of Feature Engineering

Types of Feature Engineering Strategies

Feature engineering, despite being a complex process, can be broadly categorized into four key strategies. Each of these strategies targets a different aspect of the raw data to distill valuable features. Here they are:

Feature Creation: This involves creating new features from existing ones. The idea is to impart more contextual relevance to the data. For example, you might combine two related features into one or perhaps generate a new feature by applying a mathematical function to an existing one. You might generate 'total rooms in a house' by adding 'number of bedrooms' and 'number of bathrooms'. This strategy typically necessitates a sound understanding of the domain.

Feature Transformation: In this strategy, the features are transformed into a format that's more suitable for the chosen algorithm. For instance, many algorithms work better if the distribution of values is closer to normal, so a skewed feature might be log-transformed to achieve this. Scaling features to a standard range is another common transformation, especially when the model is sensitive to the scale of the input features.

Feature Encoding: Encoding refers to the conversion of categorical data to numerical data that our machine-learning models can understand. Basic examples of encoding include turning a binary feature, like 'yes' or 'no', into 1s and 0s, or implementing one-hot encoding for nominal categories. These transformations allow models to interpret qualitative information quantitatively.

Feature Selection: Even after the successful creation, transformation, and encoding of features, not all features are equally useful for a given predictive task. Some may be redundant, or not contribute much to the model's performance, or even decrease it. Feature selection involves identifying and keeping only the most impactful features. By removing noise and redundant features, the model's performance and interpretability can be greatly enhanced, and computational efficiency can also be increased.

Each of these strategies enhances the raw data in different ways, and the importance of each might vary depending on the type of data and the specific problem at hand. As we traverse further into the realm of feature engineering, we'll explore detailed techniques pertaining to each of these strategies and discover how they reveal the hidden potential in the raw data.

Feature Engineering Techniques

Detailed Feature Engineering Techniques

Let's delve deeper into the specific techniques for handling different types of data during feature engineering:

Continuous Data: These are numerical variables that can take an infinite number of values. Common techniques for continuous data include:

Normalization/Standardization: Since different features might be on entirely different scales, normalization adjusts all features to a comparable scale by altering the range of data. Standardization transforms data to have a mean of 0 and a standard deviation of 1.

Binning: You might want to transform continuous data into discrete 'bins'. For example, instead of using “age”, you might use the category “20-29”, “30-39”, *etc.*

Polynomial Features: Using polynomial features can help capture relationships between features that aren't visible in the linear scale.

Categorical Data: This represents types or categories. Here are techniques aimed at categorical data:

One-Hot Encoding: This transforms each category value into a new feature and assigns a binary value of 0 or 1. Each category gets its own feature.

Ordinal Encoding: If the categories have an inherent order (like 'low', 'medium', 'high'), ordinal encoding can be used to preserve this information.

Ordinal Data: This is a type of categorical data with a clear ordering of the variables. While ordinal data can often be treated as either categorical or numerical data, one common tactic is to simply retain the same numeric values but treat them as categorical in your model.

Temporal Data: If you're dealing with time-series data or dates, specific techniques can be used:

Time Since: One common feature is the duration since a particular event occurred.

Cyclical Encoding: Times of day, days of week, months in a year, and other cyclical features might be best represented using a sine/cosine transformation to encode the cyclicity.

Additionally, Interaction features are created by combining multiple features. This is often useful in exposing new information that algorithms can leverage to improve the prediction.

Ultimately, the techniques used will heavily depend on your specific problem, the nature of your data, and the model you're using. Each of these methods can unveil the hidden potential in your data assets, transforming them into a gold mine of insights and predictions.

Case Study

Real-Life Example of Feature Engineering

Let's consider a real-world case in the domain of real estate price prediction. Imagine you've been tasked with building a model to predict housing prices based on a given dataset.

The raw data you have includes details like house size (square footage), number of bedrooms, number of bathrooms, age of the house, location, *etc.* While these look like useful features already, we can apply feature engineering to uncover even more insightful inputs for our model.

Feature Creation

Instead of using a number of bedrooms and bathrooms separately, we create a new feature “total rooms” by combining them.

From 'location', we generate two features - 'distance from the city center' and 'school rating in the neighborhood'.

These new features incorporate more meaningful information in a single feature.

Feature Transformation

The sizes of the houses have a wide range, but we observe from our data that predictions do not increase linearly with size. Thus, we apply a logarithmic transformation to the 'size' feature.

Feature Encoding

The feature 'location' is categorical. For a better representation, we use One-hot Encoding to convert each unique location into a binary feature.

Feature Selection

After creating several new features, we noticed that some of them do not contribute much to the target variable 'house price'. We employ a feature selection technique to remove such features, thus reducing noise and complexity from our model.

After applying these feature engineering techniques, we train our model again. The result? An observable improvement in prediction accuracy! Not just that, our model now generalizes well to new data and even gives us more interpretable insights due to the improved feature set.

This use case illustrates how judicious feature engineering transformed raw and seemingly unrelated data into meaningful predictors, thereby boosting the performance of our predictive model. It perfectly epitomizes feature engineering - the art of showcasing the beauty and value hidden in raw data! Fig. (**4**) demonstrates how various data types can be handled and transformed during the feature engineering process to improve the input quality for machine learning models.

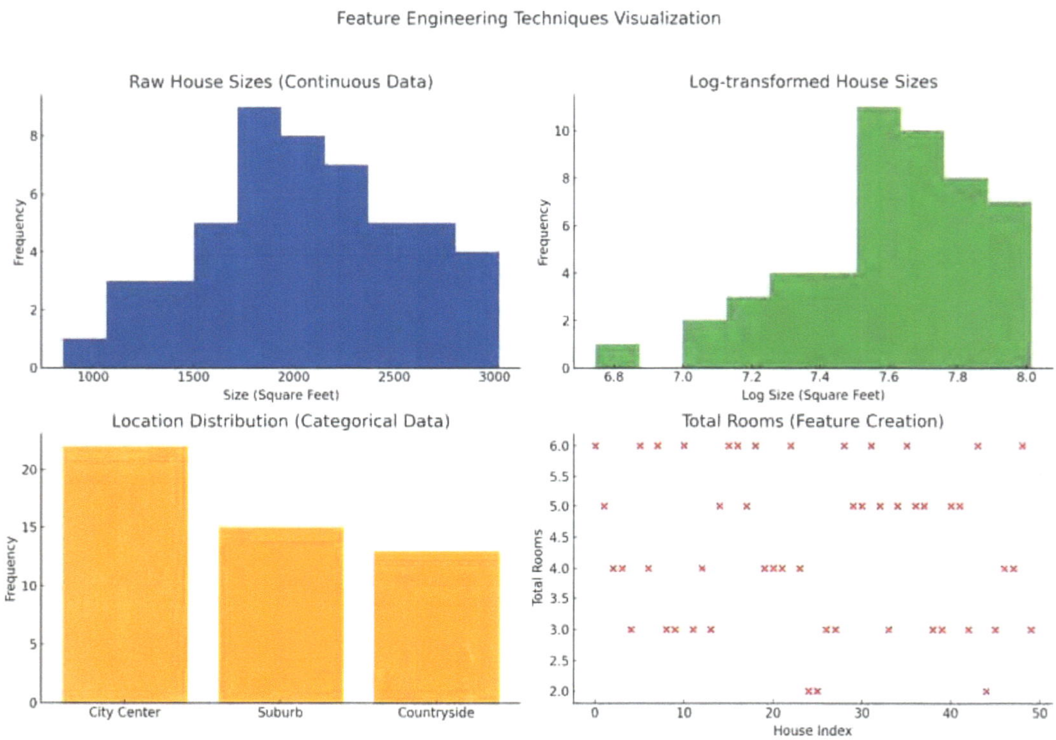

Fig. (4). Different feature engineering techniques applied to a simulated dataset. Raw House Sizes (Continuous Data): This histogram shows the distribution of house sizes before any transformation. Log-transformed House Sizes: The second histogram shows the distribution after applying a logarithmic transformation, which is useful for normalizing data and handling skewed distributions.Location Distribution (Categorical Data): This bar chart displays the frequency of each category within the location data.Total Rooms (Feature Creation): The scatter plot illustrates the total rooms in each house, combining bedrooms and bathrooms into a single feature, showing how raw data can be combined to create more insightful features.

Challenges in Feature Engineering

While feature engineering is certainly the lifeblood of any machine learning project, it is not without its challenges. Here are some pitfalls and hurdles data scientists might face while engineering features:

Dealing with Missing Values: Almost all real-world data collections encounter the challenge of missing values. Choosing the right imputation method for missing data is tricky and can impact your model's outcomes. For example, replacing missing values with the mean of a feature might not be suitable if the data is skewed or if the feature's distribution is not normal.

High Dimensionality: Sometimes, feature engineering can lead to a high number of features compared to the number of observations, resulting in a high dimensional dataset. High dimensionality can increase the computational complexity of the model, may cause overfitting, and can affect the interpretability of the model. Techniques like dimensionality reduction or regularization can help, at the risk of losing some information.

Biased Data: If your data does not represent all cases equally, but instead leans towards certain outcomes, it can bias your model's predictions. It is important to be mindful of your data collection methods and be aware of any potential biases inherent in your data.

Irrelevant Features: Introducing irrelevant or collinear features during feature creation could lead to overfitting, increased computational cost, and reduced model interpretability. Feature selection methods are there to help, but they add an extra layer of complexity to the process.

Constant Feature Adaptation: Oftentimes, once a model is deployed, the data continues to evolve and change. This means that feature engineering is an ongoing process. Features may become redundant, or new useful features might become available.

Hard to Automate: Feature engineering often demands domain knowledge, creativity, and a deep understanding of the data, which makes it challenging to automate. While there are tools and methods developed for automated feature engineering, they might not always be as effective as manual, contextually relevant feature engineering.

We can think of these challenges as an intricate part of the artistry of feature engineering. They require an inventive, tenacious, and thoughtful data scientist to work through them, further demonstrating that feature engineering is as much an art as it is a science.

Automated Feature Engineering

While feature engineering is an art, the growing field of machine learning has brought about considerable advancements in automating this process. Automated feature engineering aims to assist data scientists in creating effective inputs for their models, reducing the time spent on this stage and making the machine learning process more efficient.

Here are a few key aspects of this emerging field:

Tools and Libraries: There are an increasing number of tools and libraries designed to simplify and automate the feature engineering process. For instance, libraries such as 'Featuretools' in Python offer a framework that can automate various feature engineering techniques. These tools can automatically generate new features from your data, perform complex aggregations, transformations, and much more.

AutoML Platforms: Several AutoML platforms, such as Google Cloud AutoML, H2O's AutoML, and Microsoft's Azure AutoML, provide built-in feature engineering capabilities. These platforms not only help with automatic model selections and hyperparameter tuning but also include steps for automatic feature engineering.

Neural Network Approaches: Deep learning models, notably neural networks, implicitly perform feature engineering by automatically learning useful representations from the raw data, reducing the need for manual feature engineering. However, they are computationally intensive and require large amounts of data.

Evolutionary Algorithms: Evolutionary algorithms and genetic programming can be leveraged to 'evolve' a large number of potential features and select the most relevant ones for model training.

Despite these advancements, it is important to note that automated feature engineering does not replace the need for domain expertise and manual feature engineering. Automated processes may generate a vast number of features, but a deep understanding of the domain can guide more meaningful feature creation. As a result, automated feature engineering is often seen as a companion — not a replacement — for the manual process.

Indeed, the future of feature engineering will likely involve a blend of automated techniques and traditional, human-guided feature engineering. The goal here is to permit the machines to handle the tedious and repetitive work, freeing up the data scientist to think critically, solve complex problems, and apply their domain knowledge.

Conclusion

Emphasizing the Artistry of Feature Engineering

As we've journeyed through the process, intricacies, and uses of feature engineering, one aspect continues to underscore every aspect of it, the sheer artistry involved. While on the surface it may seem to be a technical and mechanical process, a deep dive reveals the presence of artistic elements that play a significant role in effectively crafting features.

Domain Knowledge: Understanding the domain is akin to understanding the 'mood' or the 'theme' of a piece of art. It's the basis that drives the creation of new features and gives meaningful transformation to the raw data. The understanding of how variables interact with the business problem or the prediction task is a skill that is honed over time and experience.

Intuition: An artist needs intuition to guide their creation, much like a data scientist requires it to guide their feature selection. Determining what features could be important, hypothesizing interactions, and predicting the impact of the features on model outcomes all lean heavily on the intuition of the data scientist.

Creativity: One needs creativity to synthesize raw materials into a piece of art. Similarly, a data scientist requires creativity to craft meaningful features from raw data. Whether it's creating interaction features, extracting information from dates or text, or transforming skewed data, there's ample space for creativity in feature engineering.

Critical Thinking: Critical thinking is vital to envision the end result and to overcome challenges in art. Similarly, during feature engineering, it helps in troubleshooting issues like missing data, outliers, high dimensionality, *etc.* and devising strategies to handle them adequately.

In summary, feature engineering straddles both science and art, where the science of learning algorithms is complemented by the art of presenting data in a way that helps these algorithms learn better. The blend of domain knowledge, intuition, creative problem-solving, and critical thinking makes the process of feature engineering more than a mechanical exercise, shaping it into an art form that's an essential part of the data science landscape.

THE CATBOOST WAY: TRAINING AND EVALUATION

Introduction and Background

CatBoost's Niche: Handling Categorical Features

One of the biggest challenges in machine learning is the effective handling of categorical features - those which represent a limited, and usually fixed, number of possible values. Examples might include car make (Toyota, Ford, BMW, *etc.*), color (red, blue, green), or day of the week. These are ubiquitous in real-world datasets, yet surprisingly difficult to handle well.

The traditional methods to convert these categorical features into a numerical form that machine learning algorithms can process include One-hot encoding or Ordinal encoding. However, these approaches can have certain limitations, such as increased data dimensionality or inaccurate representation of categories.

This is where CatBoost excels and stands apart from its peers. The name "CatBoost" itself is derived from two words "Category" and "Boosting". As the name implies, it is specifically designed to handle categorical variables, reducing the burden on data scientists to perform extensive data preprocessing.

CatBoost handles categorical features using a variety of techniques, but primarily by employing a method called "Mean Encoding" (or Target-based encoding). It involves calculating a statistic (usually the mean) on the target variable with respect to the categorical feature and replacing the category with that calculated statistic. While the idea is simple, it can easily lead to overfitting if not done correctly. CatBoost effectively handles this using a method called "Ordered Target Statistics" or "Ordered Boosting". It adds a random permutation to the dataset and calculates mean encoding sequentially to avoid leakage.

This unique and effective way of handling categorical features makes CatBoost a highly valuable tool when dealing with datasets with categorical features, providing better performance without extensive feature preprocessing. It's an algorithm that provides a great starting point for many machine learning tasks, and even sometimes the best ending point.

The Training Process

Ordered Boosting in CatBoost

One of the key components of CatBoost is its novel Ordered Boosting method. To understand why it's important, we first need to comprehend the problem it solves:

Target Leakage.

When dealing with categorical variables, one common approach is target encoding, which calculates statistics such as mean, sum, *etc.* of the target variable for each category. While it's quite effective, it introduces a risk. If we calculate these statistics using the entire dataset, we bring information from the future (test set) into the past (training set), causing a 'target leakage'. As a result, our model might perform impressively well on the training set (since it had access to information it shouldn't), but will likely perform poorly on unseen data.

CatBoost manages to avoid target leakage and performs target encoding through Ordered Boosting. Here's how it works:

The data is randomly shuffled and processed line by line.

When calculating the encoded feature for a row, CatBoost considers only the rows that precede it in the randomized order and excludes the row itself and following rows.

In other words, CatBoost does a form of 'leave-one-out' encoding as it passes through the training set, to avoid leakage.

This approach ensures that the target encoding is calculated without introducing information from the future, thereby eliminating target leakage and leading to more reliable models. It's this meticulous, technically sound handling of target leakage that makes CatBoost a highly robust and effective gradient boosting algorithm.

Oblivious Trees in CatBoost

While CatBoost can use standard decision trees as its base model, its default and distinguishing choice is a specific type of tree called “Oblivious Trees”.

An Oblivious Tree is a symmetric decision tree where every level of the tree corresponds to a decision on one feature. This means that each path through the tree - from root to leaf - that has the same depth also uses the same features in the same order for making decisions. Because of their symmetry, oblivious trees consider fewer features at each split compared to a traditional decision tree and therefore tend to have more levels.

Here are some key differences between Oblivious Trees and Conventional Decision Trees:

Node Splits: In a conventional decision tree, each internal node can split based on a different feature, offering high adaptivity to data. In contrast, in an oblivious tree, each level corresponds to one feature, and all nodes at the same level split on the same feature value. Despite apparently being a limitation, it has advantages in terms of computational simplicity and efficiency.

Tree Depth: As each node at the same level in an Oblivious Tree makes the same split, they tend to be deeper (more levels) than conventional trees for equivalent complex decision-making.

Computation Efficiency: The symmetric structure of Oblivious Trees allows for efficient computation. It simplifies the calculation of derivatives needed for gradient boosting and allows for vectorized operations, which significantly speeds up the training time.

Bias-Variance Tradeoff: Oblivious Trees tend to have a higher bias but lower variance compared to conventional trees. This means they might not fit the training data as closely, but they are less likely to overfit, and the performance on unseen data is often better.

The use of oblivious trees is part of what makes CatBoost exceptional. It's a testament to their innovative approach to enhancing the efficiency and performance of gradient-boosting algorithms. While they may be a bit more abstract to understand than conventional decision trees, they provide a balance of bias and variance that often leads to superior predictive performance, as shown in Table 7.

As shown in Table 7, a comparison between Oblivious Trees and Conventional Decision Trees reveals several key differences. In terms of Node Splits, Oblivious Trees split each level on the same feature, with all nodes at a level being identical, while Conventional Decision Trees allow each internal node to split based on different features. Regarding Tree Depth, Oblivious Trees tend to be deeper due to uniform splitting at each level, whereas Conventional Decision Trees have varying depths, which may not be as deep for equivalent decision-making. In terms of Computational Efficiency, Oblivious Trees feature a symmetric structure that simplifies calculations and speeds up training, whereas Conventional Decision Trees have a more complex structure that may slow down computations. Finally, with regard to the Bias-Variance Tradeoff, Oblivious Trees have higher bias but lower variance, making them less prone to overfitting, while Conventional Decision Trees have lower bias but potentially higher variance, which can lead to overfitting.

Table 7. Comparison of oblivious trees and conventional decision trees.

Feature	Oblivious Trees	Conventional Decision Trees
Node Splits	Each level splits on the same feature; all nodes at a level are identical.	Each internal node can split based on a different feature.
Tree Depth	Tend to be deeper due to uniform splitting at each level.	Depth varies; may not be as deep for equivalent decision-making.
Computational Efficiency	Symmetric structure simplifies calculations and speeds up training.	More complex structure may slow down computations.
Bias-Variance Tradeoff	Higher bias but lower variance; less prone to overfitting.	Lower bias but potentially higher variance; can overfit.

Model Evaluation and Practical Tips with CatBoost

After we've built a model using CatBoost, the next step is to evaluate its performance. The following are some ways to do this and a few practical tips to get the most out of CatBoost.

Model Evaluation

Cross-Validation: CatBoost has built-in methods for cross-validation. This technique is a robust way to evaluate a model's performance by dividing the available data into 'folds' and iteratively training and testing the model on different subsets of these folds.

Accuracy Metrics: Like most other machine learning libraries, CatBoost provides various accuracy metrics that can be used to measure the performance of the model. Depending on the problem, you can use metrics such as Logloss, CrossEntropy, AUC, Precision, Recall, F1, and many others.

Practical Tips

Use the Appropriate Objective Function: One parameter to set when training your CatBoost model is the 'loss function', or objective function. Make sure to choose the most appropriate one given your specific problem.

Hyperparameter Tuning: While CatBoost is designed to give good results out of the box, you can almost always improve performance by tuning hyperparameters. Consider the learning rate, depth of trees, regularization parameters, and others.

GPU Training: Training gradient boosting on large datasets can be time-consuming. CatBoost allows for GPU training, which can greatly accelerate this process. If you have access to a suitable GPU, this can greatly speed up your modelling processes.

Interpretability: You can use the built-in 'feature importance' method to interpret how your model is making predictions. This function calculates the importance of each feature by quantifying the improvement each feature brings to the overall result.

Remember that while CatBoost offers many advanced features out of the box, it's vital to understand your data and problem well. This understanding will not only guide your feature engineering and model building process, but it will also help inform which of CatBoost's many features you should utilize and how to interpret your results. All of these measures will help ensure you're getting the most out of your models.

CONCLUSION

The journey through model building using Catboost illustrates a comprehensive approach to extracting value from data. From the initial problem definition to the deployment of the model, each step is crucial in ensuring the accuracy and effectiveness of the predictions. This chapter not only demonstrates the practical application of the Catboost model but also highlights the transformative power of machine learning in cryptocurrency market forecasting, providing a roadmap for analysts and practitioners to follow.

Despite these strengths, the work has potential limitations. The effectiveness of the Catboost model heavily depends on the quality and diversity of the data provided, which may not always be available or sufficiently comprehensive in real-world scenarios. Additionally, the focus on categorical data, while beneficial, may overlook the nuances that other types of data could offer to the predictive accuracy and model robustness.

Future research could explore integrating multimodal data sources to enhance the robustness and accuracy of the model. Investigating the scalability of the Catboost model in other domains and refining algorithms to handle sparse or imbalanced data more effectively are also promising paths. These steps would help mitigate the limitations and expand the applicability of Catboost to a broader range of predictive tasks.

REFERENCES

Chhajer, P., Shah, M., Kshirsagar, A. (2022). The applications of artificial neural networks, support vector machines, and long–short term memory for stock market prediction. *Decision Analytics Journal, 2*, 100015. [http://dx.doi.org/10.1016/j.dajour.2021.100015]

Sheta, A.F., Ahmed, S.E.M., Faris, H. (2015). A comparison between regression, artificial neural networks and support vector machines for predicting stock market index. *Soft Comput.,* *7*(8), 2.

Siami-Namini, S., Namin, A.S. (2018). Forecasting economics and financial time series: ARIMA vs. LSTM. *arXiv preprint arXiv:1803.06386.*

CHAPTER 6

Optimizing Big Data Strategies

Abstract: Chapter 6 of "Cryptocurrency Market Forecasting with Catboost Models" examines various strategies for optimizing big data handling in the context of modern data processing and storage. The chapter explores the fundamentals of data processing techniques, the role of machine learning in enhancing data processing, effective data storage solutions, and the integration of distributed computing frameworks. It aims to provide insights into creating efficient, scalable, and robust systems for handling the vast amounts of data typical in cryptocurrency market analysis.

Keywords: Big data, Cryptocurrency forecasting, Data processing, Data storage, Distributed computing, Data compression, Data indexing, Machine learning, Performance optimization.

INTRODUCTION

This chapter introduces the critical aspects of big data strategies that are essential for processing, storing, and managing large-scale data sets effectively. It discusses the evolution of data processing methods, from traditional batch processing to real-time processing enhanced by machine learning technologies. The chapter also covers various data storage options, including on-premise and cloud-based solutions, and introduces the concept of distributed computing as a means to handle the computational demands of big data.

Previous research in this field has largely focused on optimizing individual components of data processing and storage systems, often examining them in isolation. Studies have explored various algorithms for batch and real-time processing, as well as the effectiveness of different storage architectures for scalability and security (Casado and Younas, 2015; Habeeb *et al.*, 2019).

The novelty of this research lies in its holistic approach, integrating these components into a cohesive framework that leverages cutting-edge machine learning algorithms and distributed computing technologies. By synthesizing these elements, the study aims to demonstrate improved efficiency and reduced latency in data processing and storage operations. This integrated approach also

Heng Chen

addresses the interdependencies and potential bottlenecks between data processing and storage, offering a more comprehensive solution to the challenges of big data management.

DIGITAL EDEN: SECRETS OF DATA PROCESSING AND STORAGE

Introduction to Data Processing

In the modern digital age, data has emerged as one of the most valuable assets for businesses. From understanding consumer behavior to forecasting trends, efficient data utilization can deliver insights that drive strategic decision-making. However, raw data is like raw diamonds - without proper cutting and polishing in the form of processing, it is hard to unlock its full potential.

Data processing is the method of converting raw data into a meaningful format that is easier to understand and analyze. It involves cleansing, standardizing, transforming, and sorting data so it can be used in various ways to help a business grow and make more informed decisions.

Types of Data and their Processing

In the data-saturated landscape of today, businesses handle several types of data daily:

Structured Data: This type of data is highly organized and typically stored in a database. It is easy to process and analyze. Structured Query Language (SQL) is commonly used to handle this type of data.

Unstructured Data: This refers to data in free-form text or multimedia content. Due to its lack of structure, specialized data mining and text analysis techniques are used to process it.

Semi-Structured Data: This is a blend of structured and unstructured data and could include data in XML or JSON format. APIs, NoSQL databases, and code-based processing are typically used for semi-structured data.

The nature of the data determines the methodologies and techniques for processing it.

The Data Processing Cycle

Data goes through various stages in the Data Processing Cycle:

Collection: This is the first stage of data processing where data is gathered from various sources.

Preparation: The collected data is then cleaned and transformed into a format that can be inputted into a computer for further processing.

Input: Here, the prepared data is inputted into a data processing system or software.

Processing: During this phase, the input data is analyzed and interpreted using various processing algorithms or operations.

Output and Interpretation: The processed data is translated into a meaningful format (like reports, graphs, *etc.*). It is then analyzed and used for strategic decision-making.

Storage: The final stage in the data processing cycle is storing and maintaining the processed data for future use and analysis.

In essence, data processing is the backbone of information management. By transforming raw data into a structured format, businesses can identify patterns, decode trends, and extract valuable insights that inform their strategic planning and decision-making.

DATA PROCESSING TECHNIQUES AND TECHNOLOGIES

Common Data Processing Techniques

Two commonly employed techniques in data processing are Batch Processing and Real-Time Processing.

Batch Processing: Here, data is collected over time and processed all at once. Once the process starts, it continues until all operations are performed. This method is highly efficient for large volumes of data and is less costly as it does not require significant computational power. Batch processing is commonly used in operations where real-time data processing is not required, such as payroll processing, end-of-day reports, or data backup.

Real-Time Processing: In this method, data is processed instantly as it is received, without any delay, providing real-time insights. This is particularly useful in operations that require immediate action, such as fraud detection in banking transactions, or live traffic updates in a GPS system. The trade-off for real-time insights is higher computational needs and potentially more complexity in data processing.

Machine Learning and AI in Data Processing

Machine Learning and AI dramatically enhance data processing capabilities. AI can automate data processing, sifting through huge volumes of data more quickly than manual processing could ever achieve. Machine Learning algorithms can detect intricate patterns and learn, improving the accuracy and efficiency over time. They are used for tasks such as anomaly detection, predictive modeling, natural language processing, and many more.

Popular Data Processing Tools and Technologies

Various tools and technologies cater to different data processing needs:

Hadoop: Apache Hadoop is highly effective when dealing with vast data sets across clusters of computers. It is designed for distributed storage and distributed processing using simple programming models.

Spark: Apache Spark is known for its lightning-fast analytics and ease of use for large-scale data processing. It has built-in modules for SQL, streaming, machine learning, and graph processing.

Flink: Apache Flink is a stream processing framework. It is proficient in running real-time data processing and analytics, as well as handling complex event processing.

Each of these tools brings unique strengths to data processing, and their application depends on the specific requirements, such as volume and speed of data, computational resources, and the specific data processing tasks at hand. By utilizing the right tool for a given situation, businesses can unlock the power of their data, enabling more informed decision-making and strategic planning.

As shown in Table **8**, different data processing techniques and methods serve various purposes in modern data management. Batch Processing accumulates data over time and processes it all at once, making it suitable for use cases such as data backup, end-of-day reports, and payroll processing. Real-Time Processing processes data immediately as it is received, without delay, and is ideal for scenarios like fraud detection in banking transactions and real-time traffic updates. Machine Learning and AI automate data processing by utilizing algorithms that improve efficiency and accuracy through model learning, making it applicable for anomaly detection, predictive modeling, and natural language processing. Lastly, Common Tools and Technologies such as Hadoop, Spark, and Flink are designed for large-scale data sets, distributed storage, and processing.

Table 8. Data processing techniques and methods.

Data Processing Technique	Description	Use Cases
Batch Processing	Accumulates data over time and processes it all at once.	Data backup, end-of-day reports, payroll processing.
Real-Time Processing	Processes data immediately as it is received, without delay.	Fraud detection in banking transactions, real-time traffic updates.
Machine Learning and AI	Automates data processing using algorithms and improves efficiency and accuracy through model learning.	Anomaly detection, predictive modeling, natural language processing.
Common Tools and Technologies	Hadoop, Spark, Flink	Suited for large-scale data sets, distributed storage and processing.

DATA STORAGE SECRETS

Transition to Data Storage

While data processing is a fundamental aspect of turning raw data into actionable insights, the importance of the related field of data storage cannot be understated. As the closing phase of the Data Processing Cycle, how and where data is stored has substantial implications for data management, not only in securing the data but also in making it easily retrievable for future use.

Data Storage Options

Data can be stored in a variety of ways, but we'll touch on two basic types - On-premise Storage and Cloud Storage.

On-premise Storage means storing data on local servers or hardware within your own premises. This method provides companies complete control over their data and can offer low latency. However, it may be more costly due to hardware, maintenance, and personnel expenses, and it could also occupy significant physical space.

Cloud Storage involves storing data on remotely maintained servers provided by third-party companies. Cloud storage offers high scalability, reduced IT workloads and costs, and accessibility from anywhere with an internet connection. However, firms relying on Cloud Storage must trust their provider to maintain high levels of security and reliability.

Choosing the Right Storage Solution

When selecting a data storage solution, there are several aspects to consider:

Scalability: As your business grows, your data needs will also grow. The ability to easily scale storage capacity is essential.

Security: Your data might include sensitive information that must be protected from breaches.

Cost: Storage solutions carry varied costs, including purchasing, installing, and maintaining storage infrastructure.

Accessibility: Data should be readily accessible for efficient business operations.

Compliance: Certain industries are subject to regulations regarding data storage.

Conclusion

In conclusion, effective data processing and storage form the bedrock of powerful, data-driven strategies. It is through these processes that raw data is transformed into Digital Eden – a realm of valuable insights waiting to be harvested. Businesses that effectively process and store their data are well-equipped to leverage these insights, enabling them to drive decision-making, inform strategy, and ultimately, reap the benefits of their digital assets.

THE ART OF DATA: COMPRESSION AND INDEXING

Understanding Data Compression

Definition and Importance of Data Compression

Data compression is the practice of encoding information in a format that uses less data compared to the original representation. In practical terms, it reduces the disk space required to store data and the bandwidth needed to transmit it, resulting in cost savings and performance improvements. In the era of big data, where we are dealing with a huge amount of digital information every second, data compression becomes vitally important.

Types of Data Compression

There are two main types of data compression - lossless and lossy:

Lossless Compression: In lossless compression, the original data can be perfectly reconstructed from the compressed data. It is used when it is essential that the original and the decompressed data be identical. Examples include text and data files, such as bank records and text documents.

Lossy Compression: In lossy compression, some data from the original file is discarded permanently. The result is a close approximation of the original, not an exact copy. This type of compression is used mostly for audio, video, and images, where a small loss in quality is usually imperceptible, or at least acceptable.

Role of Data Compression

Data compression plays a significant role in several industries:

- **Media and Entertainment:** Compression is vital in reducing the size of audio, video, and images without degrading perceptible quality significantly. Examples include movie streaming, music streaming, and digital TV.

- **Telecommunications:** Data compression reduces the bandwidth required for data transmission, minimizing network costs and improving speed.
- **Information Technology:** Data centers, databases, and backup systems use data compression to reduce storage requirements and speed up data transfer.

Practical Examples

Examples of data compression techniques in action are all around us:

- **JPEG Image Compression:** Digital images are often saved in JPEG format, which uses lossy compression to reduce the size of image files.
- **MP3 Audio Compression:** The MP3 format uses lossy compression to shrink the size of audio files without significantly affecting sound quality to the human ear.
- **ZIP Files:** ZIP is a file format that employs lossless compression to decrease the size of a file or folder. It is commonly used for archiving multiple files into one or making large files more manageable to send or download.

In essence, data compression is an essential tool in today's data-heavy world. By minimizing the size of our digital files, compression conserves storage space, improves transmission speeds, and allows us to efficiently navigate the digital landscape.

TECHNIQUES AND ALGORITHMS FOR DATA COMPRESSION

Data Compression Techniques

Data compression includes a wide array of techniques that fall into two main categories: basic and advanced.

Basic Techniques

- **Huffman Coding:** This is a popular lossless data compression algorithm. It involves creating a binary tree of nodes that estimate the probabilities of the different symbols (characters) in the data. The symbols that occur more frequently are assigned shorter codes.
- **Run Length Encoding:** RLE is a simple form of data compression where runs (consecutive data elements) are replaced by just one data value and count. It is generally most effective on data with lots of consecutive identical values.
- **Lempel-Ziv-Welch (LZW) Algorithm:** This is a universal lossless data compression algorithm. It builds a translation table that maps strings of input characters into codes. It is the algorithm behind GIF, TIFF, and ZIP file formats.

Advanced Techniques

- **Transform Coding:** It is a type of data compression for "source coding" (compression). It first transforms the source data into components that are more accurately and compactly presented.
- **Fractal Compression:** This is a lossy compression method used primarily for digital images. It is based on fractals and the mathematical theory of Iterated Function Systems (IFS).
- **Subband Coding:** It is a method in signal processing where the signal is split into a number of different frequency bands, and each is encoded separately.

MACHINE LEARNING AND AI IN DATA COMPRESSION

With the advent of machine learning and AI, data compression is witnessing new horizons:

- There is active research on developing AI-driven algorithms to learn the optimal compression techniques based on the type and characteristics of data.
- Machine Learning models, particularly neural networks, are being used to optimize the quality of compressed images and videos. For instance, generative adversarial networks (GANs) are often used in 'deep learning super-resolution' techniques to reconstruct higher-resolution images from compressed ones.

In summary, while basic and advanced techniques form the foundation of data compression, the integration of machine learning and AI is poised to push the boundaries further, enabling more efficient and smarter data compression strategies.

INTRODUCTION TO DATA INDEXING

Definition and Purpose of Data Indexing

Data Indexing is a technique used to improve the speed of data retrieval operations in a database. In essence, an index is a data structure that improves the speed of operations in a table. Indexing works very much like a book's table of contents - it provides a quick way to look up information, not by scanning through the entire table, but by jumping directly to the data of interest.

Importance of Indexing in Databases

The role of indexing in databases cannot be overstated. With the rapid growth in data, looking up information within vast databases could turn into a time-consuming and computationally expensive task. This is where indexing comes in. It significantly reduces the amount of data the database engine needs to examine when executing a query, leading to faster retrievals and increased performance. This speed is especially crucial for real-time applications where timely data access and performance are key.

Types of Data Indexing

Indexes come in several types, each with specific use cases:

Primary Indexing: This form of indexing is applied when the data is stored in the disk block in sequential order with a unique identification key. It is quick and efficient for lookups.

Secondary Indexing: In this case, the data is not sequential, and the index contains a pair of values with a pointer to the disk block containing the key. It is useful when access to data through non-primary means is essential.

Clustering Indexing: This is used when data is stored in the form of clusters, and each cluster has a specific range of data but may store different types of data.

Non-Clustering Indexing: This is when every single row of a column has a separate index key. It is also known as a non-unique index as it allows multiple identical values in a column.

Multilevel Indexing: It is a technique used for addressing large blocks of data. The index is divided into several levels, where the first level points to the second, which points to the third, and so on, with the final level pointing to the actual block where the data resides.

Conclusion

Both data compression and data indexing play pivotal roles in efficient data management - while compression reduces the size of data for efficient storage and transmission, indexing optimizes the retrieval of this data ensuring quick access when needed. By implementing effective compression and indexing strategies, businesses can create an effective data management system that fully harnesses the power of their data, leading to improved operations and decision-making processes.

BIG DATA WONDERLAND: DISTRIBUTED COMPUTING AND PERFORMANCE OPTIMIZATION

Understanding Distributed Computing

Introduction to Distributed Computing and Big Data

In the world of Big Data, where we deal with vast and complex data sets, traditional single-machine computing systems often fall short. This is where Distributed Computing comes into the picture.

Distributed Computing is a model in which a network of computers located in different geographical locations share computational tasks. It allows us to distribute vast amounts of data and computational tasks across clusters of computers, making it an integral part of effectively handling and processing Big Data.

Distinguishing Between Single-Node and Distributed Systems

In a single-node system, all the processing occurs on a single machine. This setup might be acceptable for small-scale data and operations, but it poses scalability issues with large datasets. As the data grows, the system may run out of storage, memory, or processing power.

On the other hand, distributed computing systems divide the data and computation tasks across multiple machines or nodes. The system can handle large volumes of data and remain unaffected by the size of the data because you can always add more nodes to the system. Moreover, if one node fails, it does not disrupt the functioning of the entire system due to redundancy in distributed setups.

The Concept and Advantages of Parallel Computing

Parallel computing, a type of computation where many calculations or processes are carried out simultaneously, is at the heart of distributed computing. Large problems can often be divided into smaller ones, which can then be solved at the same time across multiple nodes.

Advantages of Parallel Computing Include

Increased Speed: By dividing tasks, the actual time taken to process data isreduced significantly.

Complexity Handling: It allows systems to handle complicated, data-heavy operations efficiently.

High Fault Tolerance: Even if one node fails, other nodes continue processing, ensuring there is no single point of failure.

Case Study

One practical example of distributed computing is its use in the Large Hadron Collider (LHC) experiment at CERN. The LHC generates approximately 30 petabytes of data annually. This data is distributed across a global network (known as the LHC Computing Grid) of more than 170 computing centers in 42 countries, in which each center carries out a portion of the physics data analysis.

Conclusion

In essence, distributed computing effectively leverages the power of multiple machines, working together to process large-scale data in a shorter time frame. It is a vital tool in the age of Big Data, enabling efficient data processing, analysis, and insight generation.

TOOLS AND TECHNIQUES FOR DISTRIBUTED COMPUTING

Distributed Computing Frameworks

When it comes to distributed computing, two of the most popular frameworks are Hadoop and Spark.

Hadoop: Apache Hadoop is an open-source distributed processing framework that allows for the distributed processing of large data sets across clusters of computers. It is designed to scale up from single servers to thousands of machines, each with local computation and storage.

Spark: Apache Spark is another open-source distributed computing system that provides an interface for programming whole clusters with implicit data parallelism and fault tolerance. One of Spark's key features is its in-memory processing, which enhances the speed of various analytic operations.

Understanding MapReduce

MapReduce is a programming model used for processing and generating large datasets in parallel. It has two main phases: the Map phase and the Reduce phase. In the Map phase, the input dataset is divided into smaller sub-datasets and processed independently. In the Reduce phase, all the mapped data is shuffled and reduced to provide a summarized output.

Spark's In-Memory Processing Capabilities

While both Hadoop and Spark can use the MapReduce model, Spark has a distinctive edge due to its in-memory processing capabilities. While Hadoop reads and writes from disk, Spark caches computations in memory, significantly speeding up iterative algorithms and interactive data mining tasks. However, Spark may require more memory than Hadoop.

Distributed Databases - NoSQL

NoSQL databases became popular as a solution to store and process data that does not fit well into traditional relational databases. They offer distributed and fault-tolerant storage across clusters.

Cassandra: Apache Cassandra was designed to handle large amounts of data across many commodity servers, providing high availability with no single point of failure.

MongoDB: It is a source-available, document-oriented database optimized for large-scale data storage. It is excellent for document-like data structures and offers horizontal scalability.

In essence, the choice between different distributed computing frameworks and databases depends on the particular needs of the task at hand. Understanding each framework's strengths and weaknesses can help guide this selection process, ensuring that the chosen tool fits the workload characteristics.

As shown in Table **9**, several distributed computing tools and technologies are essential for processing large datasets. Hadoop is an open-source framework that provides distributed storage and processing capabilities, known for being highly scalable and using a simple programming model suitable for large-scale data processing. Spark is another open-source distributed computing system that offers fast data analytics and processing, supporting in-memory computing, which makes it ideal for data analysis tasks requiring quick iterations. MapReduce is a programming model for processing and generating large datasets in parallel, dividing data processing into Map and Reduce phases, and is applicable to both structured and semi-structured data. Distributed Databases, such as Cassandra and MongoDB, provide fault-tolerant storage solutions, with Cassandra offering high availability and MongoDB optimized for large-scale data storage.

Table 9. Distributed Computing Tools and Techniques.

Tool/Technology	Description	Features
Hadoop	An open-source framework for distributed storage and processing of large data sets.	Highly scalable, uses a simple programming model, suitable for large-scale data processing.
Spark	An open-source distributed computing system that offers fast data analytics and processing.	Supports in-memory computing, fast, suitable for data analysis tasks requiring quick iterations.
MapReduce	A programming model for processing and generating large data sets in parallel.	Divides data processing into Map and Reduce phases, applicable to structured and semi-structured data.
Distributed Databases	Examples: Cassandra and MongoDB, provide distributed and fault-tolerant storage solutions.	Cassandra offers high availability; MongoDB is optimized for large-scale data storage.

PERFORMANCE OPTIMIZATION IN DISTRIBUTED COMPUTING

Load Balancing and Data Partitioning

Load balancing aims to distribute workloads evenly across multiple computing resources, like nodes or servers, to optimize the usage of resources, reduce latency, and increase overall system throughput. This not only ensures fairness but also enhances the system's responsiveness and availability.

Data partitioning, on the other hand, is a technique in distributed systems to break up the data into smaller chunks or 'partitions' and distribute them over multiple nodes. It helps to spread the load, ensure data is processed faster, and make large datasets more manageable.

Network Optimization Strategies

Network optimization involves strategies intended to increase network efficacy in handling a wide range of traffic and workloads. This could involve techniques such as bandwidth throttling, data compression, and caching to reduce latency and speed up data transfers.

Importance of Data Locality

Data locality refers to managing the data close to the processing unit that will use it. When data and its processing are close together, data access times can be greatly reduced, speeding up the computation process. This principle underlies many distributed systems' designs, including Hadoop.

Tuning Resource Allocation

Resource allocation is an important aspect of optimizing distributed computing performance. This involves distributing memory, CPU, and I/O resources among tasks to prevent inefficient usage, bottlenecks, and system failures. Proper tuning can significantly improve the overall performance of distributed applications.

Machine Learning and Predictive Analytics for Performance Optimization

Machine learning algorithms can be used to predict future resource needs based on patterns and trends, allowing systems to prepare for increased demand. Predictive analytics can also help identify potential failures or issues in the system before they become critical, ensuring uninterrupted service and optimized performance.

In conclusion, distributed systems require careful planning and management to ensure optimal performance. From load balancing to data locality considerations, many factors contribute to an efficient system. Advances in machine learning and predictive analytics present promising new ways to navigate these challenges, driving the evolution of distributed computing towards increasingly efficient and intelligent systems.

CONCLUSION

In conclusion, effective data processing and storage form the bedrock of powerful data-driven strategies. Through these processes, raw data is transformed into a realm of valuable insights, enabling businesses to leverage these insights for strategic planning and decision-making. However, there are inherent limitations in the current approaches. For instance, the scalability challenges in distributed systems and the computational overhead associated with real-time data processing can hinder operational efficiency. Additionally, the dependence on specific technologies like Hadoop or Spark may limit flexibility as new solutions emerge.

Future research should explore the development of more adaptable distributed computing frameworks that can seamlessly integrate with emerging technologies and provide more robust fault tolerance mechanisms. Investigating energy-efficient data processing techniques could also address the growing environmental concerns associated with large-scale data centers. Furthermore, enhancing machine learning algorithms for predictive analytics will be crucial to managing the increasing complexity and volume of data more effectively.

REFERENCES

Ariyaluran Habeeb, R.A., Nasaruddin, F., Gani, A., Targio Hashem, I.A., Ahmed, E., Imran, M. (2019). Real-time big data processing for anomaly detection: A Survey. *Int. J. Inf. Manage., 45*, 289-307. [http://dx.doi.org/10.1016/j.ijinfomgt.2018.08.006]

Casado, R., Younas, M. (2015). Emerging trends and technologies in big data processing. *Concurr. Comput., 27*(8), 2078-2091.
[http://dx.doi.org/10.1002/cpe.3398]

CHAPTER 7

Case Studies: Successful Market Predictions

Abstract: Chapter 7 examines several case studies that showcase successful market predictions, drawing from a broad range of historical examples and current applications of Artificial Intelligence (AI) in financial markets. The chapter explores significant instances from history where predictions have shaped economic, social, and technological advancements. It then transitions into modern times to detail how AI and machine learning technologies are now driving predictions in the financial sector, providing insights that substantially enhance decision-making and market efficiency.

Keywords: Artificial intelligence, Algorithmic trading, Deep learning, Financial markets, Historical case studies, Investment strategies, Machine learning, Market predictions, Risk management.

INTRODUCTION

This chapter delves into the historical evolution and significant contributions of predictive practices in various fields, particularly focusing on their impact on financial markets. Beginning with transformative historical events and leading into the sophisticated algorithmic strategies of today's financial systems, the narrative sets the stage for understanding the integration of traditional prediction techniques with modern AI-driven approaches.

Historically, the field of market prediction has been enriched by seminal works that have systematically analyzed the impact of economic indicators, political events, and technological innovations on market trends (Lee *et al.*, 2018; Shah *et al.*, 2019). Scholars and practitioners alike have developed a variety of models ranging from basic linear regressions used to predict future market prices based on past data, to complex quantitative and algorithmic trading strategies that incorporate a myriad of variables to forecast market movements (Henrique *et al*, 2019; van Schalkwyk, 2024). These foundational studies have established the critical role of accurate and timely information in effective market prediction and risk management.

Embark on a captivating exploration through the pivotal chapters of human history and the revolutionary strides in technological advancements that are

Heng Chen

shaping the future of our world. This narrative begins with a journey back in time, uncovering monumental discoveries and transformative periods that have laid the groundwork for modern society. From the decoding of ancient scripts on the Rosetta Stone to the intellectual flourishing of the Renaissance and the groundbreaking shifts of the Digital Revolution, each historical case study provides profound insights into the forces that have molded human civilization.

Transitioning from the echoes of the past, the focus shifts to the present and near future, where Artificial Intelligence (AI) is redefining the landscape of financial markets. Through sophisticated computational technologies, AI is transforming how market predictions are made, enhancing decision-making, and reshaping investment strategies with unprecedented precision and efficiency. This section delves into how AI is integrated into the financial sector, its impact on market dynamics, and the ethical considerations it raises.

The innovative aspect of this research lies in its comprehensive synthesis of AI applications in market prediction, highlighting not only their current capabilities but also identifying potential gaps and areas for improvement. By integrating state-of-the-art machine learning models with traditional financial analysis techniques, this study advances our understanding of how AI can be more effectively tailored to enhance predictive accuracy and reliability in dynamic market conditions.

Together, these explorations not only recount the milestones of history and the innovations of technology but also highlight the ongoing dialogue between our past achievements and future possibilities. This narrative fosters a deeper understanding of how historical lessons can inform current technologies and strategies, paving the way for a future that is both informed by legacy and inspired by innovation.

TIME TUNNEL: EXPLORING HISTORICAL CASES

Introduction and First Case Study

Introduction

Welcome to the Time Tunnel, where we embark on thrilling journeys into our rich past and unravel the stories that shaped our world. Each historical case is a treasure trove exuding the value of time and effort that went into the making of our present and the molding of our future. By diving into these captivating sagas, we aim to understand our roots, learn from the wisdom of those before us, and draw inspiration for navigating the complexities of our current times.

Our First Historical Case The Discovery of the Rosetta Stone

As we commence our adventure into the past, let us cast our glance back to 1799, where one of the most significant archaeological discoveries of all time took place the unearthing of the Rosetta Stone.

Found by French soldiers during Napoleon Bonaparte's campaign in Egypt, the Rosetta Stone became the crucial key to deciphering Egyptian hieroglyphs, a scripted language that was a mystery until then. Carved in 196 B.C., during the reign of Pharaoh Ptolemy V, the stone carries a terse report of his coronation. Its enormous value lies in the inscription being in three forms Greek, Demotic, and hieroglyphs enabling scholars to crack the hieroglyphic code using the Greek text as a reference, thereby opening a royal path into the majestic world of ancient Egypt.

The discovery of the Rosetta Stone in 1799, during Napoleon Bonaparte's campaign in Egypt, was a pivotal moment in the study of language, archaeology, and our understanding of the ancient world, as it allowed scholars to decipher Egyptian hieroglyphs using the Greek text as a reference. The unlocking of Egyptian hieroglyphs shed light on a previously inaccessible trove of historical, cultural, and religious knowledge and provided significant insights into early human civilization. Even over two centuries later, the Rosetta Stone continues to stand as a symbol of mankind's quest into understanding our past, reminding us that knowledge often arrives in the most unexpected forms. As we continue to decipher the mysteries of human evolution and cultural development, the lessons we learn from such historical cases serve as stepping stones guiding us toward the future.

Second and Third Case Studies

Second Historical Case! The Renaissance

As we journey forward through the annals of time, we arrive in a period that forever shaped the course of human history the Renaissance. This magnificent time, stretching from the 14th to the 17th century, saw an explosion of new ideas, art, and knowledge emanating from European societies.

The Renaissance or 'rebirth' was a cultural movement that marked the end of the medieval period and ushered in an era of renewed interest in the classical knowledge of Greece and Rome. The invention of the printing press by Johannes Gutenberg around 1440 played a significant role by making books more accessible, driving literacy and learning.

This era gave birth to some of the most renowned individuals in human history, such as Leonardo da Vinci and Michelangelo, whose works still inspire and awe us today. The technological advances, scientific discoveries, societal shifts, and artistic achievements of the Renaissance laid the foundation for the modern world.

Third Historical Case The Digital Revolution

Fastforwarding to the cusp of contemporary history, our third case study brings us to the Digital Revolution. This era, beginning in the late 20th century with the advent of digital electronics, marked the shift from mechanical and analog electronic technology to digital electronics.

This revolution affected most aspects of daily life and commerce, ushering in numerous changes that still resonate strongly today. The advent of personal computers, the internet, and digital telecommunication transformed the way we work, communicate, and consume information.

Arguably the heart of this revolution was the development of the World Wide Web by Sir Tim BernersLee in 1989. This invention democratized access to information on an unprecedented scale, laying the groundwork for the information driven economy and global connectivity we see today.

As we live through the ongoing digital era, it is fascinating to consider the speed of its impact in comparison to previous historical shifts. The Digital Revolution underlines the fact that history is not just a thing of the past, but a continuous journey in which we are active participants. The exploration of these historical cases underscores the importance of understanding our past to navigate our future successfully.

Importance of Historical Cases in Contemporary Context

Parallels and Contrasts

When looking into historical cases and current events, we can draw some fascinating parallels and contrasts. For instance, the democratizing influence of the printing press during the Renaissance mirrors the role of the internet in the Digital Revolution. Both significantly increased access to information, catapulted societal shifts, and sparked unprecedented innovations.

On the other hand, the difference in pace is striking. While changes during the Renaissance unfolded over centuries, the Digital Revolution's transformations happened within decades, a testament to the accelerating pace of change in our time.

Importance of Understanding the Past

Understanding the past provides us with context, allowing us to appreciate the events, innovations, and mistakes that have brought us to where we are today. Historically informed perspective can prevent us from repeating harmful patterns, guide our present decisions, and shape a better future.

Lessons From Historical Cases

The Power of Knowledge and Information: From the Rosetta Stone to the internet, access to information has always been a driving force for progress, emphasizing the need for education and the free flow of information.

Adaptation and Innovation: The way societies during the Renaissance and Digital Revolution adopted and propelled advancements showcases our capacity for transformation and growth when faced with new ideas and technologies.

The Impact of the Individual: Figures like Leonardo da Vinci in the Renaissance, and Tim BernersLee in the Digital age, highlight the enormous influence that innovative and tenacious individuals can have on the course of history.

In conclusion, delving into historical cases is not just an academic exercise, but a profound journey that enlightens our present and illuminates paths towards our future. As we learn from our past and understand its interplay with our present, we become better equipped to create a future that is informed, considered, and hopeful.

LEGENDS OF SUCCESSFUL PREDICTIONS

Understanding Market Prediction

Introduction and Importance of Market Prediction

In the world of finance, the ability to predict market movements can be invaluable. Active market prediction aims to forecast future market trends, helping investors make informed decisions about when to buy or sell their investments. Accurate market predictions enhance portfolio performance, manage risks, and ultimately, drive profitable trading decisions.

Market Prediction – The Concept and Tools

Market prediction involves anticipating potential future trends in the prices of securities or indexes, often based on historical data and statistical analysis. It is an essential component of various trading strategies and is commonly used by traders and investors alike.

Several tools and techniques assist in market prediction:

- **Technical Analysis:** This method involves analyzing past market data, primarily price and volume, to predict future price movements. It involves various charting tools and technical indicators like Moving Averages, Relative Strength Index (RSI), and Bollinger Bands.
- **Fundamental Analysis:** This technique aims to determine a security's intrinsic value by examining related economic, financial, and other qualitative and quantitative factors. It considers factors such as the company's financial health, industry conditions, and economic indicators.
- **Market Indicators:** Indicators are statistical measures that financial market traders use to forecast price trends. Examples include the Consumer Confidence Index (CCI), Gross Domestic Product (GDP), and other economic indicators.

Role of Efficient Market Hypothesis in Market Prediction

The Efficient Market Hypothesis (EMH) states that at any given time, asset prices fully reflect all available information, implying that it is impossible to consistently achieve returns above the average market returns on a risk-adjusted basis. If the EMH holds true, market prediction would be moot as it would suggest that future market movements are based on information not yet available and are, therefore, inherently unpredictable.

However, many scenarios contradict this theory, implying that markets are not always efficient. Cognitive biases, market psychology, and nonrational behavior can lead to price deviations from their intrinsic value. With this perspective, market prediction becomes an attainable strategy where investors can leverage insights derived from various analysis tools to anticipate and potentially profit from certain price patterns and movements in financial markets. Thus, while EMH provides a basic foundation to understand market behavior, the art of market prediction often involves understanding the factors that cause markets to deviate from this theoretical ideal.

Strategies for Successful Market Prediction

Practical Strategies for Successful Market Predictions

Predicting market trends accurately is not a straightforward task – it takes a blend of discipline, understanding, and keen insight. Here are some practical strategies that can enhance your market prediction success:

- **Staying Informed About Market Trends and Global Events:** The financial markets are not isolated – they respond to all manner of global events. Politics, economic indicators, geopolitical tensions, and even sudden disruptive events can have a significant impact on market behavior. Keeping a keen eye on these macro environmental factors can provide valuable context for interpreting market movements.
- **Mastering the Art of Interpreting Indicators and Patterns:** There are many indicators and technical patterns that traders swear by. Understanding what these indicators mean – and how they predict changes in the market – can be a powerful tool. Take the time to learn about these technical analysis tools, experimenting with and refining your use of them.
- **Educating Oneself About Financial Markets:** It is imperative that you invest in your financial education to understand the forces that drive the markets. This can involve formal education, reading financial literature, attending webinars and courses, and staying uptodate with financial news. Knowledge is power – and nowhere is that truer than in financial markets.
- **Managing Emotions and Maintaining Discipline:** One of the most challenging aspects of market prediction is removing emotion from the equation. Fear and greed can often drive trading decisions more than rational analysis. Setting clear rules for when to enter and exit trades, making plans and sticking to them, and not chasing losses or getting carried away with wins can help to maintain discipline and ensure your trading strategy stays grounded in sound reasoning.

These strategies, combined with perseverance and continual learning, can greatly increase your ability to make successful market predictions. But it is important to remember that no strategy is foolproof – all market predictions involve risk and the potential for loss. Balance confidence in your predictions with a healthy respect for the unpredictability of markets and the everpresent possibility of change.

Becoming a Legend in Market Prediction

The Value of Experience and Time

Experience plays a pivotal role in becoming proficient in market prediction. As time passes, traders gain exposure to different market conditions and learn how to react under various scenarios. Trial and error, lessons learned from mistakes, and the skill of adapting strategy with changing markets are all honed over time.

Successful Market Legends

Investment titans like Warren Buffett and George Soros have been successful in predicting market trends over the years.

- **Warren Buffett**, the Oracle of Omaha, is known for his value investing strategy where he focuses on buying securities that appear underpriced by some form of fundamental analysis. His approach of investing in undervalued companies with strong fundamentals helped him create sustained wealth over time.
- **George Soros** is famous for his speculative investing style. The most notable example of his skill was the short sale of US$10 billion worth of pounds, yielding a $1 billion profit during the 1992 Black Wednesday UK currency crisis. Soros studies macroeconomic trends to make bold moves.

Each had a unique approach, yet what set them apart was their rigorous research, risk management strategies, and the patience to wait for the right opportunity.

Developing Unique Insights and 'Thinking Differently'

Following the crowd can often lead to mediocre results. Developing an independent thought process, interpreting information from a different perspective, and not getting swayed by market noise are traits that can set a market legend apart. Some of the greatest investment stories have been about people who went against the tide and made unprecedented profits.

The Importance of Ethics and Responsibility

Market prediction should not only be about profit. Ethical considerations and social responsibility are equally important. Misleading practices, insider trading, and market manipulation may lead to shortterm gains but are detrimental in the long run and can have serious legal implications. Successful prediction isn't just about being right it's also about upholding the core values of honesty, transparency, and fairness.

In conclusion, becoming a legend in market prediction is a journey that involves continuous learning, experience, unique insights, and upstanding ethics. It's about making informed predictions, managing the associated risks, and always being prepared for the unexpected twists and turns of the financial markets.

Conclusion

In the arena of market prediction, striking a balance between an art of intuition and a science of rigorous analysis is pivotal. Accurate prediction is indeed a blend of insightful experience, disciplined approach, and analytical rigor. However, market prediction should not eclipse the importance of informed decision-making. Speculation can lead to risky maneuvers, whereas an informed decision is rooted in logic, understanding, and prudent judgment.

While the ability to predict market movements with precision is a powerful tool in a trader's arsenal, it's crucial to remember that no prediction can be accurate 100% of the time due to the dynamic and complex nature of financial markets. Therefore, risk management, along with diversification strategies, should always accompany market predictions.

Moreover, continuous learning and adaptability are vital in the ever-evolving financial landscape. Markets are not stationary, and therefore, the strategies, tools, and approaches should not be stationary either. The most successful market predictors are those who remain students of the markets throughout their lives, always learning, adjusting, and evolving their strategies in response to market dynamics.

Furthermore, content around market prediction should be developed with exceptional detail and authenticity. Given the financial implications associated with market predictions, promoting accuracy, comprehensive understanding, and ethical considerations are of paramount importance.

Ultimately, becoming a legend of successful market predictions is much more than being able to foresee market trends. It's about fostering a deep understanding of market dynamics, preserving uncompromised ethics, championing a commitment to continuous learning, and maintaining a resilience that stands the test of market volatility. And who knows, with these elements in your stride, you may indeed become the next legend in market prediction.

ARTIFICIAL INTELLIGENCE IN MARKET PREDICTION

Introduction

This section explores the profound impact of Artificial Intelligence (AI) on market prediction, a domain where sophisticated computational technologies meet dynamic financial markets. AI's ability to process extensive datasets and execute complex mathematical models at unprecedented speeds and accuracies is fundamentally altering the landscape of financial analysis, trading, and investment management. By enhancing decisionmaking capabilities, optimizing portfolio management, and increasing market efficiency, AI technologies are setting new standards in the financial sector.

The Integration of AI in Financial Markets

Financial institutions and investors increasingly adopt AI technologies due to their potential to provide deeper insights and more accurate predictions of market movements. From major banks to hedge funds, AI systems are deployed to analyze market conditions, assess risks, optimize portfolios, and execute trades. This shift is driven by the exponential growth in data volume, variety, and velocity generated by today's digital economy, which traditional analytical tools are insufficient to process and interpret.

Enhancing DecisionMaking Processes

AI enhances decision-making by integrating diverse data sources, including real-time market data, financial news, global economic indicators, and even social media trends. Machine learning models, a subset of AI, learn from this data, identifying complex patterns and relationships that would be impossible for human analysts to detect. These capabilities allow traders and analysts to make more informed decisions, predict market trends with greater confidence, and manage investment risks more effectively.

The Impact on Market Efficiency and Liquidity

AI's rapid processing and reaction capabilities to market data contribute to increased market efficiency. Automated trading systems can respond instantaneously to market changes, helping maintain liquidity and stabilizing the market by providing continuous buy and sell orders. However, the rapid and widespread adoption of these technologies also raises questions about market volatility and the potential for AIdriven price distortions.

Ethical and Regulatory Considerations

As AI technologies assume a central role in financial markets, they also introduce new ethical and regulatory challenges. Issues such as data privacy, algorithmic transparency, and the potential for systemic risks need to be addressed to build trust and ensure the stability of financial systems. Regulators and market participants must consider how AI is used in trading and its impact on the market, crafting policies that promote fairness and prevent manipulation.

Setting the Stage for Deep Dives

In the following sections, we will delve deeper into specific AI methodologies such as machine learning and deep learning, examining their roles in market prediction. We will explore a variety of case studies that illustrate both the potential and the pitfalls of these technologies in realworld financial settings. By understanding these tools, we can better appreciate both the opportunities and challenges they present in the evolving landscape of financial markets.

Machine Learning Models

Overview of Machine Learning in Market Prediction

Machine Learning (ML) stands at the forefront of technological advancements in financial analysis and trading. By automating the extraction of insights from large datasets, ML models have redefined the scope and accuracy of market prediction. These models adapt and improve over time, refining their predictions based on new data, which makes them highly effective for dynamic financial environments.

Detailed Types of Machine Learning Models Used in Market Prediction

Supervised Learning

Technical Approach: Models like linear regression, support vector machines (SVM), and neural networks are trained on historical data where the target variable (*e.g.*, next day's stock price) is known. This training involves adjusting the model parameters to minimize the error between predicted and actual market prices.

Practical Use Cases: Utilized by quantitative analysts to forecast asset prices, calculate probabilities of default, and predict future trends based on economic indicators like yield curves and housing market data.

Fig. (**5**) illustrates the application of a simple linear regression model for predicting future stock prices using historical data. In the visualization: Blue Line (Actual Price): represents the actual historical prices of the stock. This line shows the real movements in stock prices over the observed period. Red Dashed Line (Predicted Price): shows the predictions made by the linear regression model. The model was trained using the previous 10 days' prices to predict the next day's price. This line demonstrates how the model anticipates future prices based on the learned trends from historical data. Green Dotted Line (10day Moving Average, MA10): This moving average smooths out price data by creating a constantly updated average price over 10 days, which is useful for identifying shortterm trends.Purple DotDashed Line (30day Moving Average, MA30): similar to the 10day MA but over a longer period, this 30day moving average helps highlight longterm trends in the stock price.

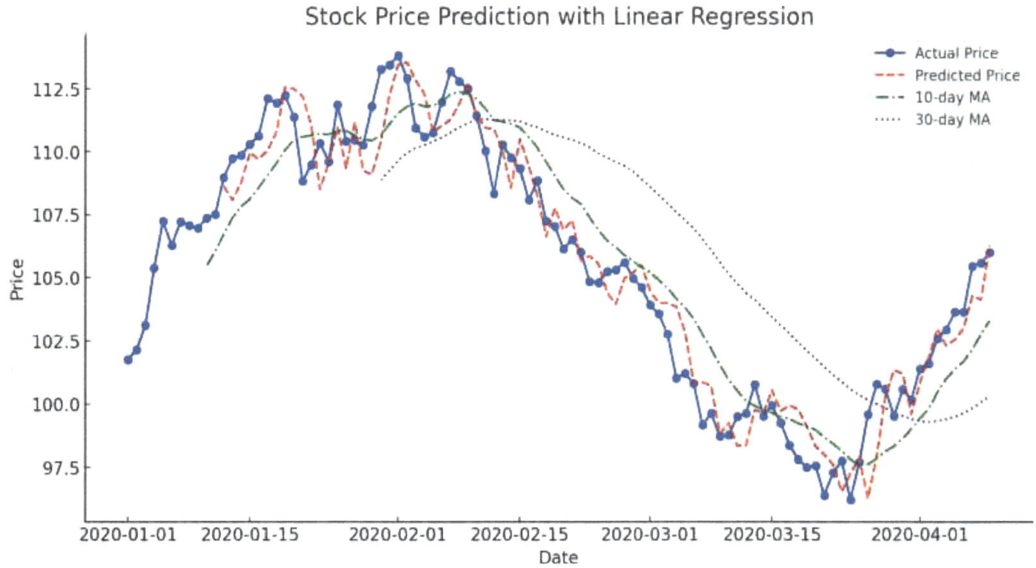

Fig. (5). Stock Price Prediction with Linear Regression

The linear regression model attempts to capture the underlying trend in the stock price data by using a window of the last 10 days' prices as features. This approach can help forecast shortterm future movements based on recent trends. Predictions are aligned closely with actual price movements but may not capture sudden shifts or anomalies due to the model's reliance on the linear relationship of past data. The moving averages provide additional context for the model's predictions, showing how the model's output compares with typical technical analysis indicators.

This model and visualization can be particularly useful for traders and analysts who rely on quantitative models to make informed trading decisions. It provides a basis for understanding how machine learning can enhance traditional stock market analysis techniques. By integrating machine learning predictions with traditional technical indicators like moving averages, financial analysts can achieve a more comprehensive analysis, potentially leading to better investment decisions.

Overall, this chart effectively demonstrates the practical application of machine learning in financial market predictions, particularly in the realm of stock price forecasting. It shows not only the capability of a simple model to predict future prices but also the utility of combining these predictions with standard technical analysis tools to enhance market trend analysis.

Unsupervised Learning

Technical Approach: Techniques such as kmeans clustering, hierarchical clustering, and principal component analysis (PCA) find patterns or group assets in data without prelabeled outcomes. These models identify hidden structures from unlabeled data.

Practical Use Cases: Asset managers use clustering to categorize stocks into different portfolios based on similarities in their returns without relying on external labels, crucial for portfolio diversification and risk management.

Reinforcement Learning

Technical Approach: Algorithms like Qlearning or policy gradient are employed where a model learns to make sequences of decisions, receiving rewards in terms of profit for correct predictions and penalties for wrong ones.

Practical Use Cases: Used to create autonomous trading systems that dynamically adjust buying and selling strategies in realtime to maximize profitability, particularly effective in highfrequency trading where opportunities may last only fractions of a second.

Advanced Applications and Case Studies

Algorithmic Trading

Indepth Explanation: Machine learning algorithms parse through terabytes of realtime trading data to detect patterns and execute trades at optimal prices, predict stock price movements, and manage large orders without significantly impacting the market.

Impact Case Study: A renowned investment firm improved its trading order execution using machine learning models, resulting in a 20% reduction in transaction costs and a significant enhancement in profit margins.

Risk Management

Indepth Explanation: ML models perform stress tests and scenario analyses by simulating various financial conditions to evaluate their impact on portfolio returns, anticipating potential future losses and suggesting mitigation strategies.

Impact Case Study: Following the 2008 financial crisis, major global banks began using advanced machine learning techniques to identify risky loan applicants and early warning signs of market downturns, substantially reducing their exposure to bad debts.

Deep Learning Impact

Advanced Feature Recognition and Time Series Prediction

Feature Recognition

Technical Details: Convolutional Neural Networks (CNNs) excel at processing visual imagery and are increasingly used to interpret highdimensional data sets in finance. These networks can automatically detect and prioritize the most relevant features from raw data, which is crucial for effective prediction in complex market environments.

Application Example: A notable case involves a major financial analytics firm using CNNs to analyze satellite images of retail parking lots, shipping containers, and global construction activity to predict economic trends. For instance, changes in the number of cars in shopping malls' parking lots can correlate with retail sales data, which is valuable for predicting stock performance of retail companies before official earnings are released.

Time Series Prediction

Technical Details: Long ShortTerm Memory (LSTM) networks and other RNNs are adept at making predictions based on timeseries data, where the sequence of data points is crucial. They are particularly effective because they can remember information for long periods, an essential trait for financial time series analysis where long-term context is key.

Application Example: Hedge funds utilize LSTMs to predict stock price movements and trade volumes by analyzing patterns in historical data. For instance, Quantitative Investment Company, a fictional hedge fund, has developed an LSTM model that analyzes years of stock market data to forecast future prices with significantly greater accuracy than traditional statistical models. This capability allows them to capitalize on market movements before they become apparent to the market at large.

Challenges and Ethical Considerations in AI-driven Market Predictions

Model Transparency and Interpretability

Issue: Despite their effectiveness, the complex nature of deep learning models can make them opaque, often referred to as “black box” solutions. This opacity can lead to trust and accountability issues, especially in highstakes environments like financial markets.

Proposed Solutions: Tools such as LIME (Local Interpretable Modelagnostic Explanations) and SHAP (SHapley Additive exPlanations) have been developed to help financial analysts and regulators understand how predictions are made. For example, a financial institution could use these tools to explain an AIdriven decision to stakeholders or regulators, demonstrating compliance with international finance regulations.

Market Manipulation Risks

Issue: There's a potential risk that sophisticated AI models could be exploited for market manipulation, creating unfair advantages and possibly destabilizing financial markets.

Proposed Solutions: Regulatory bodies are increasingly vigilant, developing frameworks to ensure ethical AI usage. For example, the U.S. Securities and Exchange Commission (SEC) has initiated programs to integrate AI monitoring tools that analyze market patterns for signs of manipulative behaviors like spoofing or pumpanddump schemes. These tools help maintain market integrity and protect investors.

CONCLUSION

The ability to predict market movements with precision is a powerful tool in a trader's arsenal, demonstrating the blend of insightful experience, disciplined approach, and analytical rigor. However, while market predictions can significantly enhance portfolio performance and guide investment strategies, they also come with inherent limitations and potential risks due to the dynamic and complex nature of financial markets.

One significant limitation of current market prediction models, including those enhanced by artificial intelligence, is their dependence on historical data, which may not always be indicative of future trends especially in volatile or unprecedented market conditions. Additionally, models often assume that market conditions observed in the past will continue into the future, which may not always hold true. This can lead to inaccurate predictions and potential financial losses.

Furthermore, the use of AI and machine learning in market predictions raises ethical concerns and regulatory challenges. The opacity of some advanced algorithms can lead to trust and accountability issues, necessitating the development of more transparent and interpretable AI models. Additionally, the potential misuse of predictive technologies for market manipulation poses a risk to market integrity.

Future research paths should focus on developing more robust models that can adapt to new market conditions more effectively and use real-time data to adjust predictions on the fly. Researchers should also work towards improving the interpretability of AI models, making them more transparent and understandable to users. Ethically, there is a need to develop and enforce stricter regulations to prevent the misuse of predictive technologies, ensuring that market predictions are used responsibly and for the benefit of all market participants.

In conclusion, while market prediction is an invaluable component of financial strategy, it is essential to balance confidence in these predictions with a healthy respect for their limitations and the ever-present possibility of change. Continuous learning, adaptability, and ethical considerations are crucial in ensuring that market predictions remain a reliable and beneficial tool in the financial landscape.

REFERENCES

Henrique, B.M., Sobreiro, V.A., Kimura, H. (2019). Literature review: Machine learning techniques applied to financial market prediction. *Expert Syst. Appl., 124*, 226-251.
[http://dx.doi.org/10.1016/j.eswa.2019.01.012]

Lee, M., Yun, J.J., Pyka, A., Won, D., Kodama, F., Schiuma, G., Park, H.S., Jeon, J., Park, K.B., Jung, K.H., Yan, M-R., Lee, S.Y., Zhao, X. (2018). How to respond to the fourth industrial revolution, or the second information technology revolution? Dynamic new combinations between technology, market, and society through open innovation. *J. Open Innov., 4*(3), 21.
[http://dx.doi.org/10.3390/joitmc4030021]

Shah, D., Isah, H., Zulkernine, F. (2019). Stock market analysis: A review and taxonomy of prediction techniques. *International Journal of Financial Studies, 7*(2), 26.
[http://dx.doi.org/10.3390/ijfs7020026]

Van Schalkwyk, P. (2024). *A machine learning framework for security forecasting and trading.*

CHAPTER 8

The Future of Market Predictions

Abstract: Chapter 8 delves into the future of market predictions by examining emerging technologies and interdisciplinary approaches that are transforming the landscape of financial forecasting. It highlights the roles of quantum computing and blockchain in enhancing predictive accuracy and introduces the integration of psychology and geopolitics into economic models. This chapter aims to provide a forward-looking perspective on how these innovations will not only refine predictive models but also reshape ethical and operational aspects of finance.

Keywords: Blockchain, Future trends, Financial markets, Geopolitics, Interdisciplinary approaches, Psychology, Predictive accuracy, Market predictions, Quantum computing, Technological innovations.

INTRODUCTION

This chapter opens with a discussion on the advanced frontier of market prediction, exploring how cutting-edge technologies and diverse disciplinary insights are converging to refine and redefine market forecasting. Historically, the field of market prediction has been dominated by quantitative models that prioritize economic and financial variables. Recent reviews of the literature indicate a growing recognition of the limitations of traditional models, particularly their inability to account for nonlinear dynamics and human behavioral factors, which are increasingly pertinent in today's volatile markets (Wang *et al.*, 2016). Researchers like Outeiral *et al.* (2021) and Fedorov (2022) have highlighted the potential of quantum computing to process vast datasets at unprecedented speeds, and Javaid (2022) has demonstrated how blockchain can ensure data integrity in financial applications.

Building upon these findings, this chapter sets the stage for a comprehensive exploration of how quantum computing, blockchain, and interdisciplinary methods such as psychology and geopolitical analysis are being integrated into predictive models, thereby enhancing their complexity and relevance in today's global financial markets. The integration of psychological and geopolitical insights represents a significant innovation in this study, moving beyond purely technical enhancements to include a broader range of human and societal factors.

Heng Chen

This approach not only addresses the technical challenges of market prediction but also incorporates a richer understanding of the external and internal influences that drive market behaviors. This research aims to create models that are not only technologically advanced but also contextually aware, providing a more nuanced tool for financial analysts and policymakers.

EMERGING TECHNOLOGIES

The financial markets of the future are poised on the cusp of a revolutionary shift, driven by breakthroughs in quantum computing and blockchain technology. These emerging technologies hold the promise of vastly enhanced predictive capabilities, far beyond what current computational methods and data management systems can offer. In this section, we explore how these technologies are not merely augmenting existing analytical tools but are redefining the very infrastructure and methodologies used in market predictions.

Quantum computing brings to the table its extraordinary processing power, capable of handling complex problems and massive datasets at speeds unattainable by traditional computers. This leap in computational ability opens new avenues for financial analysis, particularly in areas that demand intense data processing capabilities, such as real-time risk assessment, portfolio optimization, and identifying arbitrage opportunities across global markets. The quantum approach offers a significant edge in speed and efficiency, providing financial firms with the ability to make faster, more informed decisions.

Concurrently, blockchain technology introduces a paradigm of transparency and security in financial transactions and predictions. By decentralizing data storage and securing it across multiple points on a network, blockchain technology ensures the integrity and immutability of financial data. This is crucial for building trust in automated trading systems, smart contracts, and the broader financial infrastructure. Moreover, blockchain facilitates the creation of decentralized prediction markets, where collective forecasting and crowd-sourced wisdom can be harnessed to predict market movements with greater accuracy and lesser bias.

In addition to exploring the individual impacts of these technologies, this section also examines their synergistic potential—how they can interact to create more robust financial markets. For instance, quantum computing can enhance blockchain operations by speeding up the encryption processes, while blockchain can provide secure platforms for sharing the data necessary for quantum computing analyses.

Through detailed case studies and examples, we will illustrate the practical applications of quantum computing and blockchain in financial predictions. These will include discussions on projects like Project Q, which integrates quantum algorithms for market prediction, and platforms like PredictX, a decentralized finance (DeFi) platform that leverages blockchain to enhance market prediction accuracy.

As we navigate through this section, we will delve deep into how these technologies are not just evolving in parallel but are starting to converge, creating new ecosystems for financial operations and market predictions. This exploration will not only highlight the transformative potential of quantum computing and blockchain but also address the challenges and ethical considerations that come with such profound technological advancements.

As shown in Table **10**, emerging technologies are playing a significant role in market predictions. Quantum Computing is applied in portfolio optimization, enhancing the ability to analyze vast datasets simultaneously, which improves decision-making speed and accuracy, as demonstrated by Project Q. It also plays a role in market simulation, increasing the accuracy and speed of simulations for rapid response to market changes, as seen in the Financial Institution Simulation Study. Additionally, Quantum Computing is used in arbitrage opportunities to enable real-time identification and execution of strategies across global markets, as shown in the Proprietary Trading Firm Example. Blockchain technology, applied in decentralized prediction markets, increases prediction accuracy by utilizing crowd-sourced wisdom and reducing bias, as demonstrated by PredictX. Furthermore, it ensures the immutability and reliability of financial data, fostering trust in financial predictions, as evidenced by PredictX Data Verification.

Table 10. Emerging technologies in market predictions.

Technology	Application	Impact	Case Study Reference
Quantum Computing	Portfolio Optimization	Enhances ability to analyze vast data sets simultaneously, improving decision-making speed and accuracy.	Project Q
	Market Simulation	Increases the accuracy and speed of market simulations, allowing for rapid response to market changes.	Financial Institution Simulation Study
	Arbitrage Opportunities	Enables real-time identification and execution of arbitrage strategies across global markets.	Proprietary Trading Firm Example

(Table 10) cont.....

Technology	Application	Impact	Case Study Reference
Blockchain	Decentralized Prediction Markets	Increases prediction accuracy through crowd-sourced wisdom, reducing bias.	PredictX
	Data Integrity and Security	Ensures the immutability and reliability of financial data, fostering trust in financial predictions.	PredictX Data Verification

Quantum Computing

Overview

Quantum computing holds immense promise in revolutionizing various sectors, including finance and market predictions. Let us delve deeper into how quantum computing could specifically impact market predictions, with a focus on portfolio optimization, market simulation, and arbitrage opportunities, and illustrate these concepts with a detailed case study.

Portfolio Optimization

Traditional portfolio optimization involves evaluating numerous combinations of assets to find the most suitable mix that maximizes returns while minimizing risk. However, this process can be computationally intensive and limited by the capabilities of classical computers. Quantum computing, on the other hand, offers the potential to analyze vast amounts of data simultaneously, enabling more thorough and efficient portfolio optimization.

Example: Consider a hedge fund managing a diverse portfolio of stocks, bonds, and other financial instruments. By leveraging quantum algorithms, the fund can rapidly assess countless asset combinations and identify optimal portfolios tailored to specific risk preferences and market conditions. This capability enables more agile decision-making and better alignment with investment objectives.

Market Simulation

Accurate market simulation is crucial for understanding how different economic factors and events impact asset prices and market behavior. Quantum computing has the potential to significantly enhance the speed and accuracy of market simulations by processing large datasets and complex variables more efficiently than classical computers.

Example: Imagine a financial institution seeking to assess the potential impact of a sudden increase in interest rates on various asset classes. By employing quantum computing-based simulations, the institution can quickly analyze multiple scenarios and their implications for different sectors and investment strategies. This enables more informed decision-making and proactive risk management.

Arbitrage Opportunities

Arbitrage involves exploiting price differences in different markets to generate profits. Identifying and capitalizing on arbitrage opportunities require real-time data analysis and rapid execution, which can be challenging for traditional computing systems. Quantum computing offers the potential to analyze vast amounts of market data and identify arbitrage opportunities across multiple markets simultaneously.

Example: Suppose a proprietary trading firm utilizes quantum algorithms to scan global markets for price discrepancies in real time. By leveraging the speed and processing power of quantum computing, the firm can execute trades swiftly and capitalize on arbitrage opportunities before they disappear. This provides a competitive advantage and enhances profitability.

Case Study: Project Q

Project Q is a collaborative initiative between leading banks and quantum computing firms aimed at leveraging quantum algorithms for financial market analysis. One of the project's key achievements is the development of a quantum algorithm capable of accurately modeling market reactions to unexpected geopolitical events.

Example Scenario: During a geopolitical crisis, such as a sudden escalation of tensions between major world powers, financial markets often experience significant volatility and uncertainty. Project Q's quantum algorithm can rapidly analyze the potential impact of such events on various asset classes, allowing traders to adjust their strategies in real time to mitigate risks and capitalize on opportunities.

In summary, quantum computing holds immense potential to revolutionize market predictions by enabling more efficient portfolio optimization, accurate market simulations, and real-time identification of arbitrage opportunities. Projects like Project Q exemplify the collaborative efforts underway to harness quantum computing for financial innovation and risk management.

Blockchain and Predictions

Blockchain technology has emerged as a game-changer in the realm of market predictions, offering unparalleled levels of transparency, security, and decentralization. Let us delve deeper into how blockchain enhances transparency and accuracy in market predictions, and illustrate these concepts with a detailed case study focusing on a decentralized finance (DeFi) platform called PredictX.

Enhancing Transparency and Accuracy

- **Data Verification:** Blockchain's decentralized and immutable ledger system ensures that historical data used for making predictions cannot be tampered with or manipulated. This guarantees the integrity and reliability of the data, fostering trust among market participants.
- **Decentralized Predictions:** Blockchain enables the creation of decentralized prediction markets, where users can trade on the outcome of various events without the need for intermediaries. This crowd-sourced form of prediction harnesses the wisdom of the crowd, potentially leading to more accurate forecasts.
- **Transparent Audit Trails:** Every transaction on a blockchain is recorded in a transparent and immutable manner, creating an audit trail that can be verified by anyone. This transparency builds trust in automated trading systems, smart contracts, and prediction market platforms.

Case Study: PredictX - Decentralized Finance (DeFi) Platform

PredictX is a decentralized finance (DeFi) platform that leverages blockchain technology to enable thousands of users to participate in forecasting events ranging from election results to stock market movements. Let us explore how PredictX utilizes blockchain to enhance market predictions:

Fig. (**6**) displays the number of participants for two types of events on the PredictX platform: election results and stock market movements. It shows greater participation in markets related to stock market movements, indicating higher interest and engagement in financial event predictions.

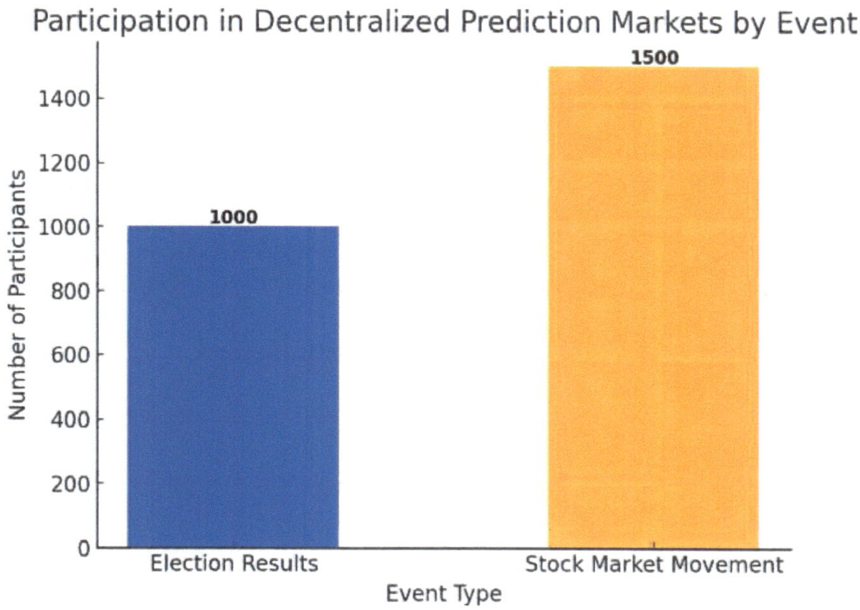

Fig. (6). Participation in Decentralized Prediction Markets by Event.

Scenario: Suppose there's a highly anticipated election in a major country, and investors are eager to gauge the potential impact of the election outcome on the stock market.

- **Data Integrity:** PredictX stores historical election data and market performance metrics on a blockchain, ensuring that the data is tamper-proof and trustworthy. Users can rely on this data to make informed predictions about the market's reaction to the election results.
- **Decentralized Prediction Market:** PredictX hosts a decentralized prediction market where users can buy and sell prediction tokens related to the election outcome and its impact on the stock market. This decentralized approach eliminates the need for centralized intermediaries, fostering trust and transparency.
- **Transparent Audit Trails:** Every transaction, including the purchase and sale of prediction tokens, is recorded on the blockchain, creating transparent audit trails that users can verify. This transparency builds confidence in the accuracy and fairness of PredictX's prediction market.

Fig. (7) shows the confidence levels for different transaction types on thePredictX platform, with numbers above each bar indicating the percentage of confidence. This highlights the platform's effectiveness in maintaining transparency and building user trust.

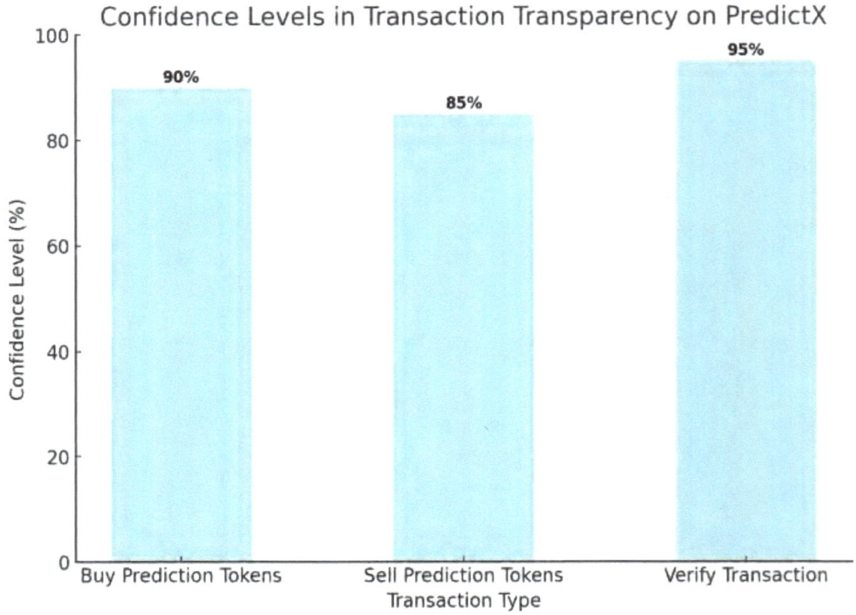

Fig. (7). Confidence Levels in Transaction Transparency on PredictX.

- **Informed Decision-Making:** Hedge funds, individual investors, and other market participants can analyze the predictions and sentiments reflected in PredictX's prediction market to make informed decisions about their investment strategies and risk management.

In summary, blockchain technology, exemplified by platforms like PredictX, is revolutionizing market predictions by enhancing transparency, accuracy, and decentralization. By leveraging blockchain's inherent features, such as data integrity, decentralized prediction markets, and transparent audit trails, PredictX empowers users to make more informed decisions in an increasingly complex and dynamic market environment.

Integrating Interdisciplinary Approaches

As the landscape of financial markets continues to evolve with increasing complexity, the limitations of traditional economic models based solely on quantitative data become more apparent. In today's dynamic market environment, a more holistic approach is required—one that integrates insights from various interdisciplinary fields to enhance the accuracy and depth of market predictions. This section delves into how integrating knowledge from economics, psychology, and geopolitical analysis can significantly enrich financial forecasting models, providing a more nuanced understanding of the forces that drive market dynamics.

Financial markets do not operate in isolation; they are influenced by a myriad of factors including human behavior, political shifts, and economic policies, which often interact in unpredictable ways. Traditional models, while useful, frequently fail to account for these complex interactions and the irrational behaviors exhibited by market participants. By incorporating principles from behavioral economics and psychology, predictors can gain insights into how cognitive biases and emotional responses influence financial decisions, leading to more accurate and actionable predictions.

Moreover, in an increasingly globalized world, understanding the impact of geopolitical events on markets is more crucial than ever. From trade wars and political upheavals to global pandemics and international treaties, each geopolitical event can have profound effects on market stability and performance. Integrating geopolitical analysis into market predictions helps financial analysts and investors anticipate market movements, manage risks more effectively, and seize emerging opportunities.

This section explores these interdisciplinary approaches in detail, discussing the benefits and challenges of incorporating these broader perspectives into market prediction models. Through examples and case studies, we will illustrate the practical applications of these approaches and how they can be harnessed to not only forecast market trends but also to understand the underlying psychological and geopolitical factors that drive these trends. By embracing a more integrated approach, financial professionals can navigate the complexities of modern markets with greater confidence and precision.

Economics and Psychology

Overview

Behavioral economics and psychology offer valuable insights into the human aspects of market behavior, shedding light on how irrationalities and emotional responses influence financial decisions. By integrating these disciplines into predictive models, we can enhance accuracy and better anticipate market movements.

Improving Prediction Accuracy

- **Psychological Triggers:** Advanced analytics now incorporate models that account for psychological triggers in market participants. These triggers include cognitive biases, emotional responses, and social influences that drive decision-making. By identifying and quantifying these triggers, predictive models can anticipate shifts in market dynamics based on collective emotional reactions to news events or economic indicators.

Example

Suppose there's a sudden announcement of an unexpected interest rate hike by the central bank. Traditional models might focus solely on economic indicators and historical data to predict market reactions. However, by incorporating psychological triggers into the analysis, a more nuanced understanding of how investors might emotionally respond to the news can be obtained. This could include fear of economic slowdown, greed for higher returns, or uncertainty about future market conditions. By factoring in these psychological reactions, predictive models can provide more accurate forecasts of market movements following the interest rate hike.

- **Enhanced Market Models:** Integrating psychological metrics into traditional financial models can provide a more holistic view of market movements, especially in highly volatile or speculative markets. By considering not only rational economic factors but also the psychological factors that drive investor behavior, predictive models become more robust and reflective of real-world market dynamics.

Example Case Study: HedgeCo

Background

HedgeCo, a leading hedge fund, recognized the importance of incorporating psychological insights into its predictive models to gain a competitive edge in the market. To achieve this, HedgeCo partnered with behavioral scientists to develop a sophisticated model that predicts stock market dips and rallies based on real-time analysis of investor sentiment derived from social media and news sentiment analysis.

Implementation

Real-time Analysis: The model continuously monitors social media platforms, news outlets, and online forums to gauge investor sentiment in real-time.

Sentiment Analysis: Utilizing advanced natural language processing techniques, the model quantifies the emotional tone of market-related discussions to identify prevailing sentiments such as optimism, pessimism, fear, or euphoria.

Pattern Recognition: By analyzing historical data alongside sentiment indicators, the model identifies patterns and correlations between investor sentiment and subsequent market movements.

Results

Outperformance: HedgeCo's model significantly outperformed traditional sentiment indicators and technical analysis methods in predicting stock market dips and rallies.

Timely Insights: The real-time nature of the analysis provided HedgeCo with timely insights into shifts in investor sentiment, allowing for proactive decision-making and portfolio adjustments.

Risk Mitigation: By incorporating psychological insights into its predictive models, HedgeCo was better equipped to mitigate risks associated with market volatility and irrational behavior.

Conclusion

The integration of economics and psychology into predictive models represents a paradigm shift in market analysis, allowing for a deeper understanding of the human elements driving financial decision-making. By leveraging advanced analytics and behavioral insights, organizations like HedgeCo can enhance prediction accuracy, mitigate risks, and capitalize on market opportunities in an increasingly complex and dynamic landscape.

Geopolitical Factors

Geopolitical events wield significant influence over financial markets, shaping everything from commodity prices to global trade policies. Integrating geopolitical factors into predictive models is crucial for anticipating market movements and mitigating risks associated with international instability.

Strategic Integration

- **Predictive Geopolitical Analysis:** By integrating AI-driven geopolitical analysis into financial models, organizations can adjust in real time to developments such as trade negotiations, wars, or international treaties. This proactive approach enables firms to adapt their strategies and positions based on evolving geopolitical dynamics, minimizing potential losses and maximizing opportunities.

Example: Imagine a global investment firm monitoring geopolitical tensions between major oil-producing countries. By leveraging predictive geopolitical analysis, the firm can anticipate potential disruptions to oil supplies and adjust its portfolio accordingly. This could involve reallocating assets away from oil-dependent industries or hedging against price volatility in energy markets.

- **Crisis Impact Models:** Predictive models that incorporate geopolitical risks can forecast the impact of international crises on market stability, providing valuable insights for firms to strategize defensive moves in advance. By assessing the potential consequences of geopolitical events, organizations can mitigate risks and safeguard their investments against unforeseen disruptions.

Example: Consider a multinational corporation with operations in regions prone to geopolitical instability. By utilizing crisis impact models, the corporation can assess the potential ramifications of conflicts, political unrest, or trade disputes on its supply chain, revenue streams, and asset values. Armed with this foresight, the corporation can implement contingency plans to mitigate risks and ensure business continuity.

Case Study: Global Analytics Inc.

Background

Global Analytics Inc. specializes in providing comprehensive risk analysis services to multinational corporations with overseas investments. Leveraging advanced AI technology, the company integrates economic forecasting with geopolitical risk assessment to offer clients early warnings of factors that could affect their international ventures.

Implementation

AI-Driven Analysis: Global Analytics Inc. utilizes sophisticated AI algorithms to analyze vast amounts of geopolitical data, including diplomatic relations, military conflicts, and regulatory changes.

Economic Forecasting: The company combines geopolitical insights with economic forecasts to assess the potential impact of geopolitical events on various market sectors and investment environments.

Early Warning System: By continuously monitoring geopolitical developments and their implications for global markets, Global Analytics Inc. provides clients with timely alerts and actionable recommendations to mitigate risks and seize opportunities.

Results

Proactive Risk Management: Multinational corporations partnering with Global Analytics Inc. benefit from proactive risk management strategies tailored to address geopolitical uncertainties.

Enhanced Decision-Making: Armed with comprehensive geopolitical insights, clients can make informed decisions regarding overseas investments, capital allocation, and strategic planning.

Improved Resilience: By anticipating and preparing for geopolitical risks, organizations can enhance their resilience to external shocks and safeguard their long-term interests.

Conclusion

The integration of geopolitical factors into predictive models represents a strategic imperative for financial institutions seeking to navigate the complexities of global markets effectively. By leveraging advanced computational technologies and interdisciplinary insights, stakeholders can enhance their predictive capabilities, mitigate risks, and capitalize on opportunities in an ever-changing geopolitical landscape. However, this convergence also underscores the importance of ethical considerations, robust regulatory frameworks, and continuous learning to ensure that financial markets remain transparent, fair, and resilient in the face of geopolitical challenges. Embracing a holistic approach to market predictions will empower stakeholders to adapt and thrive amidst evolving global dynamics.

CONCLUSION

In conclusion, Chapter 8 outlines how technological advancements and interdisciplinary approaches are profoundly transforming market predictions, emphasizing the roles of quantum computing and blockchain in refining predictive accuracy and integrating psychology and geopolitics into economic models. These innovations are positioned to not only enhance the effectiveness of financial forecasting but also address ethical and operational considerations in finance.

While these advancements promise significant improvements, it is important to recognize the potential limitations of current methodologies and the emerging technologies discussed. The inherent complexities and rapid evolution of quantum computing and blockchain may pose challenges in terms of scalability, regulatory compliance, and integration with existing financial systems. Furthermore, while the integration of psychology and geopolitics offers deeper insights into market dynamics, it also introduces additional variables that can complicate model validation and the interpretation of data.

Future research should focus on overcoming these challenges by developing more robust frameworks for technology integration, enhancing the transparency and reliability of predictive models, and continuously updating the regulatory and ethical standards that govern financial forecasting. Additionally, exploring the long-term impacts of these technologies on market stability and economic policy will be crucial. By addressing these potential limitations and pursuing these research paths, stakeholders can better harness the transformative potential of these technologies to navigate the complexities of global financial markets.

REFERENCES

Fedorov, A. K., Gisin, N., Beloussov, S. M., Lvovsky, A. I. (2022). Quantum computing at the quantum advantage threshold: a down-to-business review. *arXiv preprint*. arXiv:2203.17181

Javaid, M., Haleem, A., Singh, R. P., Suman, R., Khan, S. (2022). A review of Blockchain Technology applications for financial services. BenchCouncil Transactions on Benchmarks, *Standards and Evaluations*, 2(3), 100073.

Outeiral, C., Strahm, M., Shi, J., Morris, G. M., Benjamin, S. C., Deane, C. M. (2021). The prospects of quantum computing in computational molecular biology. Wiley Interdisciplinary Reviews: Computational Molecular Science, 11(1), e1481.

Wang, W. X., Lai, Y. C., & Grebogi, C. (2016). Data based identification and prediction of nonlinear and complex dynamical systems. *Physics Reports*, 644, 1-76.

SUBJECT INDEX

A

B

C

D

P

R

S

T

www.ingramcontent.com/pod-product-compliance
Lightning Source LLC
LaVergne TN
LVHW070952210926
848482LV00002B/188
* 9 7 8 9 8 1 5 3 0 5 5 3 1 *